Introduction

Sweet Teacher Friends,

We are excited to begin this journey through Ephesians with you. Before we get too far, there are a few things we would like you to know.

First, allow us to introduce ourselves for those who do not know us.

Bonnie was born and raised in a rural Georgia town. Studying at Southeastern Baptist Theological Seminary brought her to North Carolina. During her time at seminary, she studied Women's Ministry, but God had a slightly different plan for her to teach in a local kindergarten classroom.

Bethany was born and raised in a small town in Virginia. She studied Communications and Women's Ministry at Liberty University. The past 8 years, she has been living the city life in Florida. She recently moved to North Carolina to teach middle and high school English. Though English is a passion, Bible trumps even her love for grammar. And y'all, that's big!

Secondly, let us address how to use this study.

We will be using the English Standard Version throughout this study. When we ask you questions or provide fill-in-the-blank sections, the ESV will help you to best answer these questions and fill in the blanks. If you do not have an ESV Bible, you can use the online version found at www.esv.org.

You will also find Grace Notes throughout the study. These are QR codes that link to worship songs. You may choose to listen to these songs several times throughout the week as you study as each song correlates with the week's study.

Grace Treasured sections are also featured at the beginning of each week. These are your Scripture Memory verses for the week. We have also provided a Grace Treasured QR page at the end of the study that provides QR codes that are linked to phone images that you can choose to save as your phone background.

Lastly, you may notice some grammar baubles.

While Bethany LOVES her some grammar, we have also chosen to make our study conversational. So, yes, that means we've started sentences with conjunctions. We've ended sentences with prepositions. We've purposely used fragments in places. Bonnie thinks that's SO okay! Bethany says it's okay because as she tells her students, "If you know the rule and know you're breaking it and have a reason for breaking it, it's permissible." (Just don't apply that to life, please. haha)

Our prayer is that this study will challenge you as you experience God's grace in a whole new way and understand that grace really does change everything.

Bethany and *Bonnie Kathryn*

GOT QUESTIONS?

We tell our students that every question is a good question. Sometimes, we tend to forget to ask questions as adults. I, Bonnie, have a life statement that I remind myself of often: "If you are living, you are learning." We know that throughout this study you may have questions that will arise. Please use the QR code below to ask as many or as few questions as you would like. We will work to respond to your questions via email.

SHOPPING LIST

- ✓ Colored Pens, Pencils, Markers, Crayons, or Flair Pens
- ✓ Post-It Notes
- ✓ Bible (ESV)
- ✓ QR Reader
- ✓ Cozy Blanket
- ✓ Favorite Drink

HOW TO USE QR CODES

We both use QR codes in our classroom. QR codes are a fun way to make learning tech-based and interactive. Bethany uses QR codes for self-check in her centers. It helps her to avoid having 20 questions during an activity. It is a great way for students to self-assess. Bonnie uses QR codes for write-the-room activities, listening-to-reading activities, and to show how-to videos for handwriting. She begins the school year teaching her five-year-olds about QR codes and how to use them on the class iPads. We believe that if Bonnie's kindergarten students can use a QR code reader, so can you!

STEP 1

You will want to download a FREE QR code reader app on your iPad, iPhone, or Android phone. Do not pay for one. There are SO many free options that work well. If you find that one is acting quirky, then delete and pick another free option.

STEP 2

Open your newly downloaded QR code reader app. You will need to give it access to your camera. It will prompt you.

STEP 3

The app will have a square box that you will hold over the QR code. It should scan immediately, and it will take you to whatever the QR code is linked. Essentially, the QR links to different webpages. Throughout this study, our QR codes are linked to videos and phone images that are on Google Drive.

STEP 4

Try it out here:

Scripture Memory

Scan the QR codes and use these images as your phone background each week. We hope that seeing these on your phone each week will help in your journey to memorize Ephesians 2:1-10.

Week 1

Week 2

Week 3

Week 4

Week 5

Week 6

Week 7

Levels of Commitment

As teachers know, differentiation is necessary in every classroom. What is a challenge to some students is a breeze to others...and vice versa. During this study, you are in our classroom. So...

We would like for you to make a commitment based on the level of involvement you would like to have. We know that everybody's level of commitment is going to be different...and that is a-okay! This is not a decision that we want you to make lightheartedly, but one that we would like you to commit to prayer first. Your choice should stretch you, but not overwhelm you. On Day 1, you will record your level of commitment.

Bible Study: This level is a commitment to do the Bible Study as outlined in this book that you are holding right now.

Online Study: This level is a commitment to do the Bible Study and the weekly videos that can be found on the Bonnie Kathryn Teaching YouTube account.

Scripture Memory: This level is a commitment to do the Bible Study, Online Study, and Scripture Memory, Ephesians 2:1-10, which is recorded in the Grace Treasured sections of the Bible Study.

Writing Ephesians: This level is a commitment to do the Bible Study, Online Study, Scripture Memory, and Writing the Book of Ephesians during the 7-week study time period.

Week 1

Have you ever had a student whose behavior just baffled you? Several previous students come to mind. One of my first middle school teaching jobs was by far my hardest. I taught in a school that basically brought in inner city kids. As a young 20-something teacher, I had no idea how to handle these kids. One in particular stands out to me. I'll never forget seeing the face of this petite, little seventh grade boy turn a shade of red I had never before seen. It happened in the blink of an eye. I watched the red spread from his neck up to his forehead. Before I could say a word - or even think of how to handle the situation - he was out of his seat, trying to tower over another student who had said something that simply struck him wrong. I moved him outside quickly where I decided not to punish him, but rather to find out what was causing his quick temper. As I listened, my heart broke. This boy, new to our school, had just lost his dad in a car accident. He felt the weight of the responsibility for his mom and little sister now that his dad was gone. That day, what I saw was a little boy trying to be a man, yet his 4 foot 10 self wanted to crawl under his desk and sob because his world had been shattered. We devised a signal that day that allowed him to go outside and calm down rather than blow up in the classroom. What I learned that day was this: it is vital as a teacher to know our students' backgrounds. If we don't know what's going on at home and in their worlds - in their hearts and minds - we can't reach them as we desire.

Background matters. Paul knew that, too. He was quick to dive into the culture of those he was trying to reach in order to best serve them. He wanted to know how they did life, why they believed what they believed, why they acted the way that they acted, all to better serve them and encourage them to be who God had called them to be.

In my classroom, I never again saw an outburst from that student. He knew I cared about more than his English grade. To this day, I hear from this not-so-little boy. He's all grown up. He texts me to tell me he's doing well - working full time and still remembers all the talks we had so many years ago. Listen, I'm far from the best teacher. I have room to grow like every other teacher, but one thing that student taught me (and many more at that school like him if I'm honest): our grace meter is off when we don't know someone's background. Will you join us then to learn more about Paul's background? He was king of searching out the backgrounds of those he served, so I think it would behoove us to stop and take this week to learn a little more about the one who "[became] all things to all people, that by all means [he] might save some" (1 Corinthians 9:22).

DAY 1
Grace Notes

The Lord is My Salvation

Grace Treasured

And you were dead in the trespasses and sins in which you once walked.
Ephesians 2:1-2a

This is where we begin our journey. Wait. Do not pass GO. Do not collect $200. First, you must make your commitment as to which level you are going to commit this summer. Circle your level below then write a statement of your commitment in the "I promise…" box.

LEVEL ❶   LEVEL ❷   LEVEL ❸   LEVEL ❹

I promise

We teach our students that knowing a book's characters helps us to comprehend what we are reading. The Bible is not any different. Let's take a moment and characterize Paul. Most scholars would agree that Paul wrote the book of Ephesians.

On the next page, you find a characterization bubble map. Below each bubble is a Scripture reference where you will find more information about Paul. In the bubble, record one or two words that tells us who Paul was. You can take moment to color the picture of Paul because face it…we know you really want to color. Don't deny it!

Paul

Ephesians 1:1
Hint: What is his title?

Acts 22:3
Hint: What was his education?

Acts 22:27-28
Hint: Where was he born?

Acts 21:39
Hint: What did he call himself?

Paul was born to a devout Jewish family.

"…⁴though I myself have reason for confidence in the flesh also. If anyone else thinks he has reason for confidence in the flesh, I have more: ⁵circumcised on the eighth day, of the people of Israel, of the tribe of Benjamin, a Hebrew of Hebrews; as to the law, a Pharisee…" Philippians 3:4-5

Paul was a Roman citizen.

He was a Jew with Roman citizenship, which would later serve well in reaching both Jews and Gentiles with the Gospel. To be a Jew and Roman citizen was a big deal.

Paul was well-educated.

Paul studied the Torah under Gamaliel. Gamaliel was a well-respected leader in the Jewish community. He was recognized as the educator of educators by Christian and non-Christian historians. He would be the Ron Clark of Biblical times. Paul was fluent in Hebrew and Greek — and some say Latin as well. Dude was smart.

Paul was an apostle.

An apostle is someone who was with Jesus and learned from Him during His earthly ministry. Paul was an apostle because he had seen the Lord after His death and resurrection - just as the 12 disciples. Read 1 Corinthians 15:3-10.

Vocabulary to Know

Jew: from the tribe of Judah; one of the tribes of God's chosen people; a nationality.

Gentile: a nation of people; essentially, anyone who is not a Jew

Torah: first five books of the Bible

If anyone could have bragging rights, Paul could have. His background, education, pedigree, and experience would have given him "permission" to brag. However, he says, "for whatever I gain, I count as loss compared to knowing Christ Jesus...but by the grace of God I am what I am..." Paul does not take credit for who he is or what he has done - he recognizes it is the work of God's GRACE in his life.

Grace Point

Spend a few moments in prayer asking God to help you recognize the work of His grace in your life.

DAY 2

Bethany says that any good English teacher knows that a good reader is not only going to study the author's background, but is also going to look at the audience the author is trying to reach. With that said, read Ephesians 1:1 and determine who Paul's audience was and what one adjective he used to describe them.

AUDIENCE

_____

ADJECTIVE

_____

Where are they located? _____

Yes, the letter of Ephesians was written to the saints of Ephesus. Ephesus was a happenin' place, but not happenin' in the right way. It was a port city, which brought lots of commerce to the area. It was a melting pot of religion where many religious scholars lived and visited. Ephesus was home to many different religious temples, including the well-known temple of Artemis, a fertility goddess. Most of these temples would have had a form of prostitution as an act of worship. The ministry of Paul would have been a huge threat to this way of life. Bottom line...this place was downright sinful. Not Jesus friendly. Not family friendly. Not Jesus in the workplace friendly.

Tell us again, how did Paul describe the people of Ephesus?_____

Even in the midst of this type of culture, they were considered faithful. Many of us may face environments where it can be hard to be faithful to Christ. It may be your home life. It may be where you work. Paul's letter challenges us not to forget who we are in Christ and live out the life that God has called us to live.

Where is it hard for you to be faithful right now?

Just like the people of Ephesus, we may face situations that cause us to have gospel amnesia. We forget who we are in Christ. Paul's letter was intended to remind the faithful in Ephesus of their true identity in Christ. We could sum that up in one word:

The kindergarten teacher, Bonnie, says you need to color this. :-)

Before we go any further, we need to define the word that Paul used to describe his audience: faithful. There are two definitions for faithfulness. We believe that Paul considers both definitions when he mentions this characteristic of the people of Ephesus.

Definition 1: People who show themselves faithful in the <u>transaction of business</u>, <u>execution of commands</u>, and the <u>discharge of official duties</u>.

Definition 2: People who have been persuaded that Jesus has been raised from the dead and that He is the Author and Finisher of salvation.

Look up Galatians 5:22-23. Galatians is the book before Ephesians and was also written by Paul. So...just turn back one page.

We read in those verses that faithfulness is one characteristic of a godly person given to us by the Holy Spirit, which means that knowing God is the first step to being faithful to God.

We know as teachers that kids need a good foundation. We strive day in and day out to provide our students with a solid foundation. Paul knew that the GOSPEL was and still is the foundation for living a life of faithfulness. In fact, in every letter that Paul writes, you will find the foundation of the Gospel clear as day. In the book of Ephesians, it is found in Ephesians 2:1-10. Did someone say Scripture memory verses? Hehe.

Let's let Paul be our guide down the Romans Road.

1. **Romans 3:23** "For all have sinned and fall short of the glory of God."
2. **Romans 6:23** "For the wages of sin is death, but the free gift of God is eternal life in Christ Jesus our Lord."
3. **Romans 5:8** "But God shows his love for us in that while we were still sinners, Christ died for us.
4. **Romans 10:13** "For everyone who calls on the name of the Lord will be saved"
5. **Romans 10:9-10** "Because, if you confess with your mouth that Jesus is Lord and believe in your heart that God raised him from the dead, you will be saved. For with the heart one believes and is justified, and with the mouth one confesses and is saved."

Everywhere you see a traffic cone, write one truth from each verse from the Romans Road.

To know God personally means putting faith and trust in the Lord Jesus Christ. We must understand that there is nothing we can do to earn salvation. Salvation comes from grace alone, through faith alone, in Christ alone. Having come to faith in Christ, we are now able to grow in our relationship with Christ. Faithfulness is cultivated in our lives as we grow in godliness. The people in Ephesus knew their foundation, who they were in Christ, which allowed them to remain faithful in the midst of a worldly culture.

Answer Key: 1. We are all sinners. 2. The penalty for sin is death. 3. Jesus paid our penalty. 4. If you call on the Lord, you will be saved. 5. Confession plus belief equals salvation.

DAY 3

Yesterday, we took the time to define faithfulness. Paul described the people of Ephesus as faithful. The people in Ephesus remained faithful in the midst of a worldly culture. However, that was not always the case...

Look up Revelation 2:2-4.

Did you get that? Did you read vs. 4? To make sure you caught it, write vs. 4 below.

Jesus was speaking through John to the church of Ephesus, telling them to go back to their first love. Though they were faithful, something happened to cause their faithfulness to diminish. It is possible that they got wrapped up in their worldly culture, but to be good scholars of God's Word, we cannot assume that their culture is what caused them to "lose their first love."

A little brain snack: It's a good rule of thumb when studying scripture not to try to fill in the gaps when God's word does not specifically spell out something. God's word is inerrant and infallible, meaning it has everything we need to know inside the books written. Making assumptions is dangerous. 2 Timothy 3:16-17

Let's take a look at what might hinder faithfulness in our lives. Many different things may cause our faith to be hindered. The root of those things is the same: sin.

We are fighting a constant battle between following our flesh and following the Spirit. When we choose to follow our flesh, we choose sin, and therefore find that our faithfulness is hindered.

So...what is sin? Sin is what separates us from a holy God.

Lying.
Laziness.
Overworking.
Overeating.
Undereating.
Selfishness.
Adultery.
Gossip.
Disrespect.
Hypocrisy.
Lack of Self Control.

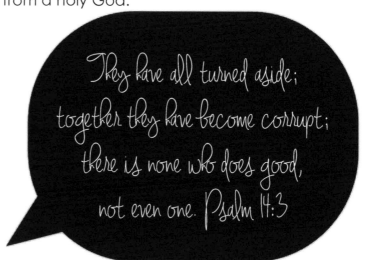

They have all turned aside; together they have become corrupt; there is none who does good, not even one. Psalm 14:3

The Bible is clear that no one is righteous. We all sin. We are born sinners. You don't have to teach a child how to sin. You don't teach a toddler to shout "MINE!" It comes naturally.

At the root of all sin is pride, and pride is an idol. An idol is something we bow down to instead of bowing down to God. Until we can recognize these idols in our lives, we will continue to bow down to them.

It is easy to blame Satan for our sin. But let's be real...while he is happy with our choice to sin, it is ULTIMATELY our choice to sin. Don't give Satan more credit than he is due.

Take a moment to write down or reflect on areas of sin in your life that are a battle for you.

A healthy view of our sin helps us to have a healthy view of our Savior. If we believe that sin in our lives is small, then our need for a Savior is small. However, the more clearly we can see sin in our lives, the more clearly we recognize our great need for a Savior. If there ever comes a point where we think, "Hey! I'm doing all right," then we have reached a dangerous point of disillusionment.

"Remember therefore from where you have fallen: repent, and do the works you did at first..." Revelation 2:5a

Jesus was ultimately calling the people of Ephesus to repent for leaving their first love. Repent literally means to do an about-face. Turn and walk away.

Let's pray together to ask God to reveal to us areas of sin in our lives that are causing faithfulness to be hindered.

Father,
Open my eyes to see areas of sin in my life that may
be hidden and hindering my faithfulness to You.
May I be faithful to You in how I speak to others,
care for my family, make life decisions, and serve
You as a teacher. I love You, Lord.
Amen.

DAY 4

Phew! Aren't you glad yesterday is over!?! We don't know about you, but yesterday wore us out! It was certainly a heavy topic.

Faithfulness should be a consistent part of every area of our lives.

We must be faithful to God in our relationships.
We must be faithful to God in our work.

Relationships.

Practically speaking, being faithful to God in relationships means prioritizing others' needs before our own. This past school year, our school adopted the theme "I am Third." We emphasized that our lives should follow the pattern of "Jesus, Others, Self."

Look up Philippians 2:3-4. Write it below.

What does this mean?

Husbands: It means putting your husband's needs - and we mean all of them - before your own needs EVEN if your husband is not treating you in the same manner or with respect. Speaking of respect: men need respect from their wives.

Faithfulness is not dependent on how someone else behaves.

Children: It means putting down the phone.

Story time.

Bonnie has a neighbor that is notorious for leaving her blinds pulled up. The home is wide open for the world to see. Bonnie lives in a somewhat urban area. We often joke about how this neighbor truly lives in a fish bowl. One night, Bonnie came home and could clearly see her neighbor sitting on her couch talking on the phone. Her cat was DESPERATE for attention and proceeded to try to crawl between her and the phone. The neighbor swatted the cat away. A couple of minutes later, she tried to pick up the cat. As we all know, cats are finicky. The cat wanted absolutely nothing to do with her. He squirmed his way out of her arms and ran away. Though a bit of a stretch, perhaps, this cat is much like our children. We are consumed with household chores, phones, TV, and many other distractions. We swat away our children, and when the time comes for us to want a relationship with them, they may just swat us away.

Faithfulness to our children also means that we are primarily responsible for their discipleship and growth. It means stopping during those teachable moments to disciple their hearts. Family quiet time and Scripture memory is a part of this discipleship as well.

Practically speaking, what does this look like for your family or future family?

(If you are thinking, "This doesn't apply to me right now," just wait. It is coming later in this study.)

Family: Our family knows the good, the bad, and the ugly about us. Faithfulness to family may sometimes mean forgiveness, even when we feel like someone may not deserve to be forgiven. Remember forgiveness is more about your relationship to God than it is about the issue you may have with someone else. We have to be willing to forgive them, knowing that Christ forgave us for so much more than we deserve.

Faithfulness to God in this area means making sure that having relationships with our family is a priority. We both live away from our extended families. However, in the culture of the school where we teach, many of our coworkers and students live just down the street from each other. At our school, we have 2 coworkers who are sisters-in-law. Each Sunday night, their family gathers to eat dinner together. They make it a priority to be involved in each other's lives.

While not everyone may be able to have Sunday night dinner, it is still possible to make relationships with family a priority. For Bonnie, it means FaceTime conversations with family and periodic trips home. I, Bonnie, am the first to admit that I don't call my dear sweet Aunt Dianne and my dear Grandmother like I should. For Bethany, it means group text messages on a daily basis.

How does faithfulness to your family practically play out for you? Is there someone that you need to forgive or with which you need to make an effort to build a better relationship?

Friends/Coworkers: Forgiveness applies in this area as well. How easily do you forgive a coworker for sinning against you? Do you harbor resentment against them? It is important to remember that just like our students, we don't necessarily know what is going on in someone else's life, so we need to err on the side of grace when dealing with our friends and coworkers.

Just as important as forgiveness is choosing to celebrate a coworker's success even if you aren't feeling particularly as successful as you would like to be. We are sure most of us have been in a situation where we may have been passed over for a promotion or recognition. Do we choose to celebrate our friend's success, or does our heart harbor resentment?

List some practical ways that you can choose to encourage a friend or a coworker.

Work.
Look up Colossians 3:17, Colossians 3:23-24, and 1 Corinthians 10:31.
What theme do you see running through these verses?

Ultimately, we do what we do for the glory of God. We are working for Him, not man. This means it does not matter who is watching, what kind of recognition we receive or do not receive, or even if we like our current job.

When I, Bonnie, first started in the teaching world, my school did not have a full time teaching position for me. This meant that my afternoons were devoted to aftercare. In order for me to have full time employment, I had to work aftercare. While there were some joys of aftercare, it was not my favorite. I LONGED for a classroom of my very own. I spent year after year feeling like I was in a holding pattern and daydreaming of the day I would be able to have a full time teaching position. God had to teach me to be content in the situation I was in at the time. Eventually, I was able to move out of aftercare and into a full time classroom. However, as I look back on that time period of my educational career, I can see how God was teaching me how to build parent and student relationships. He allowed me time to learn from other teachers. I now lovingly call one of them my "coach." My classroom would not be what it is today without my "coach" and the time I spent in the aftercare world.

You may not be in a position at work that you want. However, we must remember that God never puts us in a holding pattern unless He has a purpose. Learn to be content where you are right now. If you don't learn the art of contentment now, even your "ideal job" won't bring contentment. It is a heart issue.

The same could be said for:

Singleness.
Barrenness.
Joblessness.

Remember the idols we discussed in day 3? These desires are idols, too. Until we learn to see them for what they are, we will never truly learn to be content.

Record a time in your life where you weren't exactly where you wanted to be. This could be something in the past or your present situation.

Our desire is to be faithful to God in all areas, but ultimately, it begins with faithfulness in our relationship with God. Remember Revelation 2:2-4? Yeah. Now would be a good time to re-read those verses.

Go ahead.

What was God's ultimate goal for the people of Ephesus?

We read that He wanted them to get back to their first love. What area in your personal walk with the Lord have you neglected?

Dear teacher friend, we implore you to do exactly what Jesus commanded the Ephesians to do: REPENT and get back to your first love.

Grace Day

My grace is sufficient for you, for my power is made perfect in weakness..
2 Corinthians 12:9a

Week 2

I, Bethany, love my middle school babies...just don't tell them I called them babies! Haha However, if there is one thing I've noticed about those sweet kiddos of mine, it is this: they are chameleons. Middle school years are tough. You don't know exactly who you are. You're not sure how to figure out who you are. So what's a 12, 13, or 14 year old to do? Try on different "outfits" until they find one that fits justtttttt right like baby bear and his porridge or Cinderella and her glass slipper.

I will never forget when I started teaching older kiddos after teaching preschool babies for several years. I had a girl, we'll call her Erica, who weekly changed who she was. One week, she came to school decked out in bright colors and a smile on her face. Quite literally, one week later, she came dressed in all black, bangs hanging in her face, staring at the ground all day long. Typically, this might be reason for concern, but the very next week, lo and behold, she changed it up again. This time, she chose middle-of-the-road colors - beige, army green, burgundy - and hung out with the skater crowd. Today, when I see her posts, I smile because she looks like your average early 20-something girl. She's confident. She's beautiful. She knows who she is. Back in 8th grade? She had no clue.

Aren't you and I like Erica when it comes to our identity sometimes? We stare into our spiritual closet and wonder if we can put on the "Jesus truly loves me for me" graphic tee. We start to grab our "I am forgiven" tee but then remember the slight bauble from yesterday when we angrily shouted at our kids because it was Friday, and heaven knows by Friday, teachers' nerves are shot! We want to grab that "His grace is sufficient" shirt, but is it? Because this trial right now just makes us say "I don't know."

You aren't alone. The Ephesians struggled with this #identitycrisis too. They had no idea who they were because the world around them shouted at them to conform. "Be like us!" they said. "It will be fun!" "Bow down to our idols! They'll take care of you!" "Go your own way...be your own god. It's worked for us." The world surrounding the Ephesians was so like our world, it's not even funny. Thank goodness, we do NOT have to listen to the lies.

Paul reiterates to the Ephesians who they are in Christ. I need to be reminded of these truths often, and I'm sure you do too. So grab one of those tees from your spiritual closet. Actually, grab them all because they all speak truths about you and who you are in Christ. Join us as we dive into Ephesians 1 this week and remember WHO we are because of WHOSE we are.

DAY 1
Grace Notes

I Choose Jesus

Grace Treasured

Following the course of this world, following the prince of the power of the air, the spirit that is now at work in the sons of disobedience—
Ephesians 2:2b

Something that Bonnie always tells her students is that "learning is hard work." The Growth Mindset has become a popular teaching method in the past few years. Helping students to believe and buy into the idea that "learning is hard work" is a part of the Growth Mindset mentality. Through Growth Mindset, we teach students to embrace challenges and help them understand that challenges help them grow. This week, the tables will be turned, and you are now the student. This week learning will be hard.

There will be things that you are not able to wrap your brain around. THAT IS OKAY! In fact, that is expected. Our dear friend Paul even asked "…Who has known the mind of the Lord, or who has been his counselor?" (Romans 11:34)

Our pastor, J.D. Greear, used a great illustration in a recent sermon on Ephesians 1. He asked the question: which is greater - the gap between the mind of a 4-year-old and you or the gap between our minds and God's? Of course the answer is the second option. This is the reason that we won't be able to wrap our brains around all of this. We are not meant to fully understand everything about God and His ways.

With that said, we are going to try our best to explain the coming Scripture and be faithful to the original meaning of Paul's words. However, our dear Pastor is a better theologian than the two of us combined. We encourage you to listen to his sermon on Ephesians 1:1-14 this week during your study time. The sermon is about 40 minutes, but it is one of the best sermons on this passage that we have ever heard. We both walked away with a better understanding of a passage that we have wrestled with over the years. We will also spend more time on this during our video time together. With that said, let's roll up our sleeves and dive into this text.

J.D.'s Sermon

Look up Deuteronomy 29:29.

To whom do the secret things belong?

What belongs to us?

There are things that we know.
There are things that we cannot know.
There are things that we are not meant to know.

Read Ephesians 1:3-14 out loud. **Teacher Note:** Reading out loud helps some learners to better comprehend what they are reading.

One of Bethany's favorite things to teach is grammar. She is a nerd. However, grammar flows into literature. When we understand grammar, it is easier to understand the literature we are reading. The Bible is no different. It is highly beneficial to stop and look at the grammar when studying any passage of the Bible. If you don't know where to start when studying Scripture, using grammar is a great place.

In Bethany's English classroom, they color code grammar to help it stick. Our brains respond more to color than black and white. So, get out your colored pencils, flair pens, markers, highlighters...whatever floats your boat. Go get them. It's grammar time! (We hope some of y'all caught that pun...we are so corny.)

On the next page, we have given you some verses we want you to color-code. Using the color key below, follow the steps provided. Try it on your own first. If you get stuck on one, skip and go to the next arrow. At the end of the activity, you can scan the QR code for the answers.

Nouns = green
Verbs = yellow
Adjectives = blue
Adverbs = orange
Prepositions = purple
Conjunctions = pink
Interjections = red

 Underline the 2 subjects (nouns) at the beginning of vs. 3.
(Grammar Hint: a subject is who or what the sentence is about)

 Put an S above both subjects.

 Still in vs. 3, double underline the action verb that comes AFTER the subjects that tells us what God, our Father, did.
(Grammar Hint: an action verb is something you can do)

 In vs. 4, double underline the action verb that tells us what He did
(Hint: It's within the first 4 words.)

 In vs. 5, double underline the action verb that tells us what He did (Hint: It's within the first 3 words.)

 In vs. 7, underline the Direct Object (noun) and the noun that follows it that tell us what we have in Him (Hint: 1 starts with an r and 1 starts with an f) (Grammar Hint: a Direct Object is the person or thing that receives that action from the verb)

 In vs. 11, underline the Direct Object (noun) that tells us what we have obtained in Him.

 In vs. 13, underline the adjective (for Bethany's English nerds, the Predicate Adjective/Participle) that tells us what happened after we believed.

^{3} Blessed be the God and Father of our Lord Jesus Christ, who has blessed us in Christ with every spiritual blessing in the heavenly places, ^{4} even as he chose us in him before the foundation of the world, that we should be holy and blameless before him. ^{5} In love he predestined us for adoption to himself as sons through Jesus Christ, according to the purpose of his will, ^{6}to the praise of his glorious grace, with which he has blessed us in the Beloved. ^{7} In him we have redemption through his blood, the forgiveness of our trespasses, according to the riches of his grace, ^{8} which he lavished upon us, in all wisdom and insight ^{9} making known to us the mystery of his will, according to his purpose, which he set forth in Christ ^{10} as a plan for the fullness of time, to unite all things in him, things in heaven and things on earth. ^{11} In him we have obtained an inheritance, having been predestined according to the purpose of him who works all things according to the counsel of his will, ^{12} so that we who were the first to hope in Christ might be to the praise of his glory. ^{13} In him you also, when you heard the word of truth, the gospel of your salvation, and believed in him, were sealed with the promised Holy Spirit, ^{14} who is the guarantee of our inheritance until we acquire possession of it, to the praise of his glory.

Give yourself a pat on the back! We know that was difficult. However, we know that as we continue this study, you will find it fruitful.

One of the reasons why it was so difficult is because in Greek, these verses are ONE sentence! That's enough to make any teacher shudder.

When analyzing literature, Bethany asks her students the author's purpose for using the types of sentences they choose to use. This would be no exception. So why would Paul use ONE gigantic, humongous, wordy sentence? The answer is more simplistic than the sentence itself: he is describing everything God has done for us and given to us as His chosen ones. It's ONE idea; it's not a bunch of separate actions. When we receive salvation, we get ALL of this: we are blessed, chosen, redeemed, forgiven, adopted, and sealed.

Grace Point

Spend a few moments in prayer thanking God for His ONE massive gift.

DAY 2

Remember last week when we mentioned that the Ephesians had gospel amnesia? They had forgotten who they were in Christ.

Paul opens this letter by reminding them that they are blessed, chosen, redeemed, forgiven, adopted, and sealed. Over the next couple of days, we are going to examine these truths and see how they apply to us today.

Read Ephesians 1:3-14.

Yesterday, we had you mark the subjects. What were the 2 subjects that you marked? Write them below.

What did we say the definition of a subject was?

Paul is making a pretty profound statement in verse 3 by showcasing God as the subject of the next 6 verses. Salvation is about Him, not us.

He blessed us.
He chose us.
He redeemed us.
He forgave us.
He adopted us.
He sealed us.

 Blessed

In this verse, when Paul says blessed, this is what he means: to cause to prosper, to make happy, to bestow blessings on, favored of God. Well-known theologian, Matthew Henry, says, "He freely gives spiritual blessings, but that is not so with temporal."

What do you think Matthew Henry meant when he said this?

He means that our minds are to focus on heavenly things, not temporary earthly things. Put purple parentheses around "in the heavenly places" on Ephesians 1:3 in the passage we provided in day one. Remember the present circumstances of the Ephesians. Paul was reassuring them that though current circumstances looked less-than-blessed, they had EVERY spiritual blessing that they could ever need or want.

Chosen

Around Easter time in my (Bonnie) kindergarten classroom, we go through the resurrection eggs. I take one day to open each egg and discuss it as a class. I use it as a sequencing activity, and the kindergarten students practice retelling the story. On this particular day, we were covering the crown of thorns. Struggling to wrap her mind around why a sinless God would have to suffer and why Jesus' enemies would have treated Him so mean, one of my sweet babies simply said with a perplexed and disturbed look, "But I don't understand this." I responded to her and said, "Well, sweetheart, you are young, and some things are hard to understand. That is okay. Do you love Jesus?" She immediately responded, "OH, YES! I DO! I love Him so much!" My response to her was, "I know you love Jesus, and He loves you. Some things you will understand better as you grow up, and some things you may never understand, but we know that God loves us, and we love God. That is the most important thing."

Let's look at this AMAZING truth about being chosen.
(We hope that you have already listened to this week's song. If not, now is a good time to do so.)

• The God of the universe first chose you.
• He pursued you before the foundation of the world.
• He knew your sin and yet still chose you.
• He sent his Son so that you could have a relationship with Him.

That is HUGE and POWERFUL. Which one of these four truths encourages you the most? Write it here.

For some, this second spiritual blessing perplexes and perhaps even disturbs them because they cannot fully understand or wrap their minds around being chosen. In fact, both of us have wrestled with this truth at some point during our walks with Christ. However, this is where we become the child in Bonnie's classroom, and God looks at us and says, "I love you, and it is okay that you don't understand everything about Me. I created you in My image but with a finite mind. You are not meant to understand everything about Me right now."

Go back and re-read Deuteronomy 29:29. If it tickles your fancy, write the verse here.

27

There are secret things, and there are revealed things. Understanding everything about being chosen falls under the category of secret things. Instead of trying to fully comprehend something that is not meant for us to understand right now, let's take a few minutes to watch a video that will remind us of how BIG the God is that chose us to be His.

DAY 3

Today would be a good day to curl up with your Bible and a good cup of coffee, a hot cup of tea, a diet coke, or whatever beverage brings you joy. We will be having coffee. We wish that we could sit in your living room with you talking about this precious passage.

We have four more truths to cover today from Ephesians 1:3-14. Before we go any further, list the two we covered yesterday. Then take a moment to re-read Ephesians 1:3-14.

He_____

He_____

He redeemed us.

He forgave us.

He adopted us.

He sealed us.

 Redeemed

Let's define redemption.

Redemption is deliverance. It is freedom that has been purchased. Freedom not only from the penalty of our sin, but from its misery.

Sin in our life can certainly make us miserable. Can you a remember a time where a certain sin or group of sins made you miserable? Write that time below or take a moment to think about it.

Paul was reminding the Ephesians that Jesus paid the penalty of their sins on the cross to redeem them. They were no longer under condemnation or wrath because of sin. They were free from sin's power to rule over their lives.

→ Forgiven

All of us can probably remember a time in our lives where we had a big debt to pay off and didn't know where the money was coming from. Debt is a HEAVY burden to carry. Owing a debt you can't pay sits like a weight on your shoulders. Not having enough money in your bank account to survive feels the same way.

I, Bonnie, can remember when I first started out as a teacher. There was a week where I was praying that I would have enough gas in my car to make it to work. I didn't have enough money in the bank to afford gas. I am sure most, if not all, of us can relate to that feeling.

Sin is a debt that can weigh heavily on us. Sin separates us from a holy God. If it were not for Jesus, God's precious and only Son, we would have no relief from this debt. In God's grace and mercy, He sent His one and only Son to be the payment for that debt, knowing we could never pay it on our own. Jesus died in our place so that we could be freed from ever having to pay the debt for sin that we owe.

Forgiveness is not just a release from bondage. Forgiveness is letting someone go as though he or she never owed a debt, as though sin had never been committed. We don't know about you, but that thought is humbling and freeing at the same time.

 **Adopted**

We are not just forgiven; we are adopted by the God of the universe. Adoption is a beautiful picture of the gospel. We are certain that at least one of you have been adopted or have adopted a child. Orphans have no heritage, no inheritance, and no family. Adoption changes everything. Instantly, they are given a heritage, an inheritance, and a forever family. Isn't that beautiful?

When you are adopted, these rights become yours immediately. They're not yours for the future. They're yours right now. That is what Paul was trying to remind the Ephesians. They had access to a wonderful inheritance the moment they believed.

The moment we believe, we, too, have access to our Father's inheritance. We also get a new name.

In your favorite color, underline the four names we are given that Paul lists in 1 Peter 2:9.

1 Peter 2:9

But you are a chosen race, a royal priesthood, a holy nation, a people for his own possession, that you may proclaim the excellencies of him who called you out of darkness into his marvelous light.

 Sealed

Okay, where are my English peeps?? Bethany here.

We need to dive back into grammar for a quick sec. The word sealed is in the passive voice. Bonnie says I have to explain what passive voice is. Bless her kindergarten heart. So #grammartime!

Passive simply means that the subject of the sentence has NOTHING to do with the action it receives.

For example, if I say: The window was broken by the ball. The window did nothing to deserve being broken. The ball did the breaking. That is passive. If I say: The ball broke the window. The ball did the breaking, so it's active.

We have NOTHING to do with being sealed. God gave us the Holy Spirit, who seals us. So what does it mean to be sealed?

When kings sent a letter, they would use their signet ring to stamp their seal into hot wax to be sure the receiver knew it was from them and no one had tampered with it.

Our seal is much the same. Our Father, the King of Kings, has imprinted His name on our foreheads so that everyone, including Satan, knows we are His. When something is imprinted, it can't be removed. Our salvation is secured by this seal. It cannot be taken from us.

Jesus says in John 10:28, "I give them eternal life, and they will never perish, and no one will snatch them out of my hand."

Circle the words "no one."

That sounds signed, sealed, and secured to me.

We know that God is not going to UNseal us, UNforgive us, UNredeem us, UNinherit us, UNadopt us, or UNchoose us. While that is bad grammar, it is GREAT theology!

So who are you in Christ?

Finish these statements:

I am _____

I am _____

I am _____

I am _____

I am _____

I am _____

Grace Point

Spend a few moments in prayer thanking God for your identity in Him.

DAY 4

As we were writing this study, we spent much time praying over how to best communicate truths from God's Word. We prayed specifically that "the eyes of your hearts [would be] enlightened." Paul prayed this same prayer in Ephesians 1:15-23 for the people of Ephesus. He knew that what he had just reminded them in verses 3-14 may have been difficult to fully comprehend, so he prayed for their understanding.

Let's go ahead and read Ephesians 1:15-23.

We know that everything in Scripture is **deliberate** and **on purpose.**

Why do you think Paul chose to pray for them AFTER he reminded them of who they were in Christ in verses 1:3-14?

If we were to go back to the original Greek, we would not see these verses divided into sections or chapters.

What are the first three words of vs. 15?

These three words help us to connect verses 3-14 and 15-23. The reason Paul prayed for the Ephesians after verses 3-14 is because he knew they needed the Holy Spirit to help them fully understand what he had just told them.

"that the God of our Lord Jesus Christ, the Father of glory, may give you the Spirit of wisdom and of revelation in the knowledge of Him." Ephesians 1:17

Circle the word knowledge.

In the Greek, this word comes from the word ginosko. This word does NOT mean fact-based knowledge.

Example:
- I have 28 kindergartners in my class.
- A subject is who or what a sentence is about.

This word DOES mean experience-based knowledge.

Example:
- I knew that I wanted to be a teacher, but my first year in the classroom with REAL children was ginosko.
- I heard that a full moon turns students into crazy people, but my first time experiencing this was fo' sho' GINOSKO!!! #teacherlife

We know as teachers that kids learn best through experience. Watching chicks hatch is far more impacting than reading a book about the life cycle of a chick. Knowing and experiencing the truths about our identity in Christ is what this prayer is all about.

Let's look a bit closer at Paul's prayer for the Ephesians.

"having the eyes of your hearts enlightened, that you may know what is the hope to which he has called you, what are the riches of his glorious inheritance in the saints, and what is the immeasurable greatness of his power toward us who believe, according to the working of his great might."

 Underline the words "eyes of your hearts enlightened" in red.

 Draw an arrow from "that you" to "may know."

 Underline the three things that we "may know."
(Hint: all three are after the word "what")

Paul prays that hearts would be enlightened to understand these three truths that we just marked.

"you may know what is the hope to which he has called you"

What is biblical hope? Biblical hope is looking forward to something with great anticipation, knowing that it will happen. Because Jesus died on the cross, I know that everything I experience has a purpose. The Good. The Bad. The Ugly. The bottom line is that Biblical hope should change our outlook on life - that is our calling. This is why we can have joy in the midst of suffering.

"God is with you, even when there is no evidence that He is."

-James Merritt

"what are the riches of his glorious inheritance in the saints"

So what is this glorious inheritance that we are promised? The glorious inheritance is heaven and all the blessings that Jesus is preparing for us. This glorious inheritance also gives us direct access to communicate with a holy God in heaven and on earth.

Look up and read Philippians 3:20.

Where is our citizenship?

This means that we have to remember that we were created for heaven. This life we have on earth is just a blip on the radar.

"Only one life to live, twill soon be past, only what is done for Christ will last."

-CJ Studd

"and what is the immeasurable greatness of his power toward us who believe, according to the working of his great might."

God's power is SO great, ginormous, vast, huge, gargantuan...SO BIG that Paul did not have words that were adequate enough to describe it. Go back and circle the word that he used to describe the greatness of God's power.

That same power is at work in us and available to us through the Holy Spirit. The Holy Spirit is our helper. He helps us with this power to:

Overcome Sin.
Make Decisions.
Have Peace.
Experience Joy.

just for fun

Paul closes his prayer with an amazing, comforting truth. Why don't you go read Ephesians 1:20-22.

These verses remind us of God's sovereignty. He is the controller of ALL things. There is nothing that can enter our lives over which He does not have power. Eventually, every knee will bow and every tongue will confess that He is Lord and Savior.

Paul believed in the power of prayer. Prayer was like breath to Paul. What would happen if we prayed like Paul for our family, our coworkers, and our students? Take a moment to pray. Use Paul's model and insert the name of the person for whom you are praying.

"having the eyes of _____ {heart} enlightened, that _____ may know what

is the hope to which he has called _____ what are the riches of his glorious

inheritance in the saints, and what is the immeasurable greatness of his power toward

_____ who believe{s}, according to the working of his great might."

Grace Day

My grace is sufficient for you, for my power is made perfect in weakness.
2 Corinthians 12:9a

Week 3

I, Bonnie, believe we can learn volumes from observing the faith of a child. Children are always eager to learn more about the God who created them. They love with their whole hearts. Over the course of the school year, I watch my kinders grow in their faith. It is an honor as their teacher to be a part of their discipleship and growth. At the tender age of five and six, many of them begin to realize how their sin separates them from a holy God. Part of discipling these babies is making sure they are learning truth from a young age.

There is a Christian saying we often hear in church or around other Christian friends. We tell children that they need to ask Jesus to come and live in their hearts. Theologically, this is not an accurate statement.

Why? Because Jesus doesn't come to live in our hearts in the way a little kinder's mind would think.

Kids, being literal thinkers, will believe that a little Jesus is sitting inside their hearts. However, salvation is not one little prayer asking Jesus to live in our hearts. Salvation comes from belief in Christ, confession, repentance, continued faithful discipleship, and understanding that salvation is not about us, but rather about the finished work of Christ on the cross. It's so much more than the idea of a little Jesus in our hearts.

I once had a kindergarten student who loved Jesus with his whole heart. He was eager to learn more about Jesus and wanted to please God. One day after our Bible lesson, he crawled into my lap and got inches away from my face, like kindergarten friends so often do. He said, "Ms. Hunter, I asked Jesus if I could go live in His heart." My sweet friend had turned the statement of "asking Jesus into your heart" to a statement that put Jesus at the center...right where He should be. This little friend had a more accurate picture of salvation.

Salvation is quite simply: Jesus at the center of it all.

You see salvation is not about us finding God. Salvation is about God's pursuit of us. The God of the universe first chose you and me. He pursued us before the foundation of the world. He knew our sin yet still chose us. He sent his Son so that we could have a relationship with Him.

Jesus is the center.

He is the center of our salvation.
He is the center of our hearts
He is the center of our lives.

This week as we dive into one of Paul's most cross-centered passages, take a moment somewhere along the way to thank Him for His sacrifice of His one and only Son that He willingly gave so that we might have eternal life. Remember that nothing you can do can make God love you any more or any less. Your sin was covered on the cross. It is finished.

Choose this week to live with the heart of Christ, or as my little friend said, choose to live "in His heart," keeping Him at the center.

DAY 1
Grace Notes

[QR code]

The Lamb of God

Grace Treasured

Among whom we all once lived in the passions of our flesh, carrying out the desires of the body and the mind, and were by nature children of wrath, like the rest of mankind.
Ephesians 2:3

This has to be one of my all time favorite passages in Scripture. LIKE EVER. Bethany and I are excited about the richness of the word that is to come. We love it so much that we thought it to be VALUABLE for you to memorize during the course of this study.

Every good story contains characters, conflict, setting, plot, and theme. In the plot of most movies, there is a character or characters that are in some sort of distress. Typically, one character becomes the hero and rescues a damsel in distress. In this Gospel story, we are the damsels in distress who need rescuing. Jesus is the Rescuer.

In week one, we focused on character and audience. This week, we are going to focus on the conflict and theme, not only for the book of Ephesians, but for the entire Bible. The main conflict is what English teachers refer to as a man vs. God conflict. Sin keeps us in conflict with a holy God. It separates us from Him. However, the theme of Scripture gives us hope because the theme, or message, of the entire Bible is that a Rescuer, Jesus, has been sent to rescue us from our sin.

Open your Bible and read Ephesians 2:1-10.

"And you were dead in the trespasses and sins"

➡ Circle in blue the adjective that describes us before salvation.

➡ In purple, put parentheses around the prepositional phrase.

Paul quickly introduces the conflict: sin. As you just circled, sin is the death of us. Sin alienates us from a holy God. The very nature of God cannot be near sin.

We are all born sinners. Nobody has to teach kindergarteners to fight over their place in the line. Nobody has teach a student how to cheat on a test. Nobody has to teach us how to be jealous of someone else. Nobody has to teach us how to have a bad attitude.

The problem is that sin is usually fun for a season.

I have heard the saying, "Grass is always greener over the septic tank." That is the perfect definition of how sin may appear in our lives. On the outside, sin can be very enticing, and everything appears to be normal. However, underneath sin is a bunch of poop.

Look up and read Hebrews 11:25. How is sin described?

While sin is pleasurable for a time, its pleasures are fleeting.

"in which you once walked"

➡ Draw a stick person over the verb.

Mud baths can be cleansing at the spa, but not so much in our spiritual lives. This verse literally means that you are wallowing in the mud of your sin. Picture a pig rolling around in the mud. This is what we look like as we live in sin.

Read Luke 15:11-32

What did the prodigal son long to eat?

If you are at a point in your life where you think pig food sounds appetizing, you've reached the end of the pleasures of sin and entered into an all time low. At this point in the plot, what you are really searching for is a rescuer. If you have seen someone at this point, you probably wanted to shout, "DON'T EAT THE PIG FOOD!!!"

"...we all once lived in the passions of our flesh, carrying out the desires of the body and the mind..."

➡ Underline the words that describe in what we once lived. (Hint 5 words)

➡ Underline the words that tell what we carried out. (Hint 8 words)

"[Living] in the passions of our flesh" literally means to seek things that are forbidden.

Sin is the great ⬜Problem.
I do what I want to do.

When I am constantly sneezing and coughing, I don't say "I have a sneeze and cough." I say, "I have a cold." In other words, I don't define my sickness by its symptoms; I look for the root issue. Sin is much like this. Many believe that sin is simply defined as certain actions or behaviors; however, these behaviors are really just symptoms of a congenital sickness we've had since birth: pride. Pride is the iProblem. We believe we have it all figured out, so we put ourselves in control and try to lead our own lives. This is never anything but disastrous. The problem with pride, though, is that we often don't see it in ourselves. We need the "eyes of [our] hearts enlightened" by the great I Am, who is our Savior and Rescuer.

Grace Point

Take a moment to ask God to show you areas where you may have an iProblem. Thank God for sending his Son, Jesus, to be your Rescuer from sin.

DAY 2

"Conjunction junction, what's your function? Hooking up words and phrases and clauses..." Today's passage contains the greatest conjunction of ALL TIME.

Read Ephesians 2:1-10.

Circle in pink the conjunction that begins verse four.

"⁴But God, being rich in mercy because of the great love with which he loved us, ⁵even we were dead in our trespasses, made us alive together with Christ - by grace you have been saved - ⁶and raised us up with him and seated us with him in the heavenly places in Christ Jesus, ⁷so that in coming ages he might show the immeasurable riches of his grace in kindness toward us in Christ Jesus."

Yesterday, we looked at our iProblem: sin. We learned that sin alienates us from a holy but loving God. We also learned that because of sin, we need a rescuer. Verse four gives us great reason to celebrate because we see that God has sent our Rescuer. His name is Jesus.

He is the King of all kings.
He is the Lord of all lords.
He is our Savior.
He is our Redeemer.
He is the Sin Destroyer.
He is in control of ALL things.
Jesus is our Rescuer.

Though this is not great grammar again - starting sentences with conjunctions never is - it is GREAT THEOLOGY. Were it not for that "BUT GOD," we would still be wallowing in our sin.

Why would God rescue us? Underline the reason in verse four. (Hint: It is after the conjunction because.)

He sent us the gift of salvation because He is rich in mercy. He loves us just because he loves us. Why does a mother love her child? Just because. God the Father is the same.

just because.

In yellow, circle "were dead." What tense is the verb "were:" past, present, or future?

This word "dead" is literally translated "corpse." We were not in the process of dying. We were - past tense - DEAD. We needed resuscitation. Jesus breathed life back into our dead bodies.

Put a { } around the word "grace."

When someone has to be resuscitated, they depend fully on their rescuer. They can't help in the process. The same is true with salvation. We did nothing to help Jesus, our Rescuer. It is all about that grace!

He did all of this so that His glory and His great name would be known.

In blue, circle the word that describes His riches.

They are immeasurable. In kindergarten, my (Bonnie) kids are always amazed when I tell them that numbers never stop. They can't quite wrap their minds around numbers that never end. It is like the Energizer bunny; it just keeps going. God's grace is like this, too. We cannot measure the amount of grace that God pours out upon us.

Grace Point

Spend a few moments coloring the next page while you reflect on Jesus, our Rescuer.

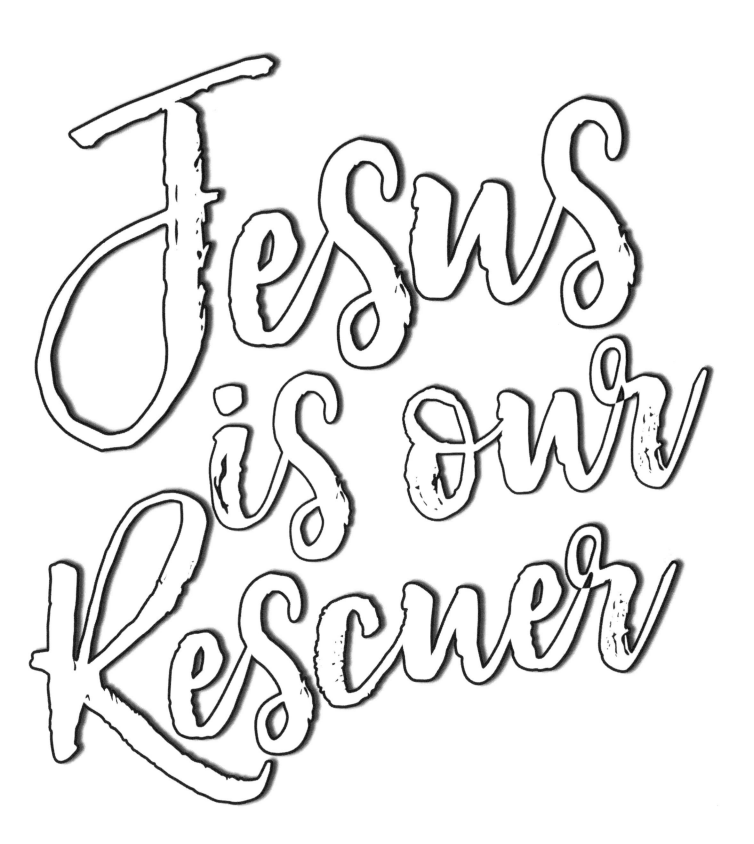

DAY 3

Let's begin today by re-reading Ephesians 2:1-10.

"⁸For by grace you have been saved through faith. And this is not your own doing; it is the gift of God, ⁹not a result of works, so that no one may boast. ¹⁰For we are his workmanship, created in Christ Jesus for good works, which God prepared beforehand, that we should walk in them."

Let's review. Looking back at your notes from yesterday, what does verse 8 mean?

Salvation is a gift that was given to us through God's grace. Faith was the only part we had in it; we simply had to believe.

Unfortunately, many people concoct a to-do list of good deeds they believe will help them earn and keep God's grace and salvation.

Look up Romans 11:6, and if you are itching to use your favorite pen again, write it below.

Paul is discussing salvation by grace here as well as in our Ephesians 2 passage. If salvation comes from our works, what do we no longer have?

In Ephesians 2:9 above, underline the reason that God didn't base our salvation on works.

If works were at the center of salvation, Jesus would no longer be the center, and the center is His rightful place. Again, we repeat: He did all of this so that His glory and His great name would be known.

So...where do good works fit into the Christian life?

In verse 10, underline what we were created for in Christ Jesus.

These good works should flow out of the love we have for our Rescuer, Jesus. Why do you do nice things for your family...your husband...your children...your students...? If it is from a true heart of love, you don't want anything in return. You simply do it out love - just because.

The good works that we were created to do should be a natural outflow of love for our Savior. We don't do them because we want to earn something; we do them because we love Him.

In yellow, circle the verb in the last 3 words of verse 10.

I think we've heard that word before. Oh wait! We have! Go back and read Ephesians 2:1-2. Where were walking then?

In the Venn Diagram below, list the difference(s) you see in verses 1 and 10 when it comes to our walking. We've started you off by giving you the one similarity.

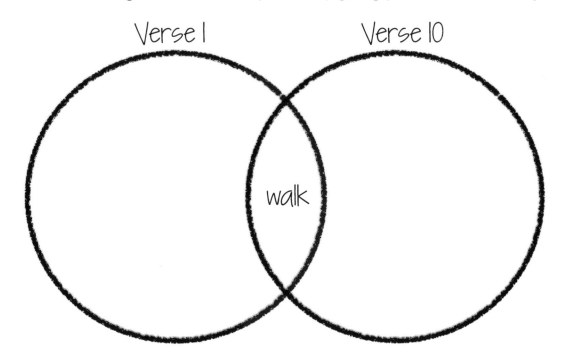

We were once like pigs, wallowing in the mud of our sin, but now, we are daughters, walking in the good works our Father has prepared just for us.

Grace Point

Spend a few moments brainstorming ways you can serve the people in your life through good works. Here are a few categories from which you may choose, or you can come up with your own: family, husband, students, boyfriend, coworkers, children, parents, grandparents, extended family, strangers, church family, etc.

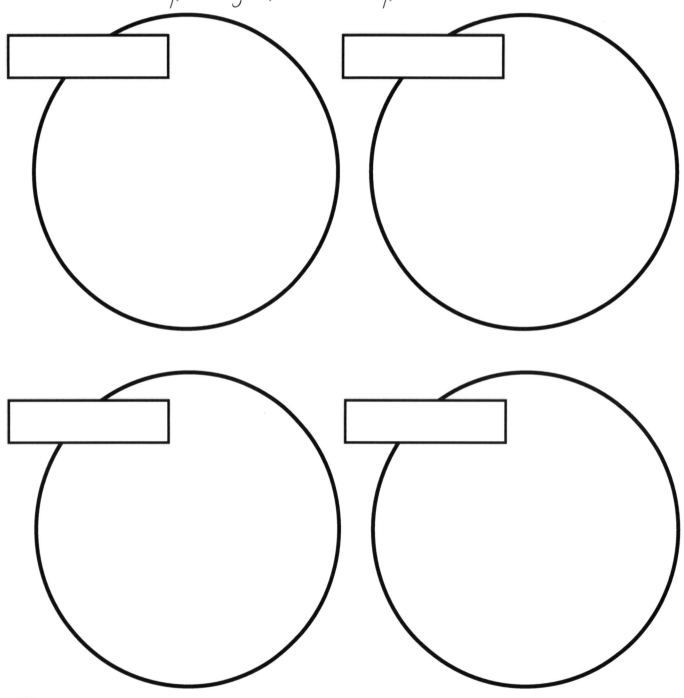

DAY 4

The past few days, we have reflected on the power that the cross has over destroying sin. Today, we are going to look at something else the cross destroyed.

Read Ephesians 2:11-22.

"16...might reconcile us both to God in one body through the cross, thereby killing the hostility."

In green, underline what else was killed on the cross with sin.

Paul is reminding the Ephesians that Jesus' death on the cross made salvation available to everyone, not just the Jews. Remember, Paul would have understood the hostility between the Jews and the Gentiles. Our society knows a similar hostility among races, socioeconomic status, and gender. You see, the Gospel is our only hope for being at peace with God — AND the Gospel is our only hope for being at peace with one another.

"14For he himself is our peace, who has made us both one and has broken down in his flesh the dividing wall of hostility."

On the wall, graffiti write some things that may divide us in our world today.

In verse 14 above, underline what God did to the dividing wall of hostility.

In verse 14, circle the word "peace" in blue.

This word literally means "to join." Jesus' death on the cross joined us — no matter our race, socioeconomic status, or gender — into one family.

"¹⁹ So then you are no longer strangers and aliens, but you are fellow citizens with the saints and members of the household of God."

Look up John 13:35. How did Jesus say that people would know that we are His?

What does this practically look like in our lives?

This means we put others first. Jesus. Others. Us. We consider the needs of others before we consider our own needs. It means we put aside differences, so that our witness will be maintained and the good news of the Gospel will be proclaimed — ultimately, King Jesus will be honored. Jesus at the center.

Grace Point

Spend a few moments thanking God for breaking down the wall of hostility. Pray about ways that you can be peace in the midst of hostility - to further the Gospel. Ask God to show you areas in your life that you may be the reason for hostility.

Vocabulary to Know

Witness: the way you represent Jesus

Gospel: Jesus came and lived a perfect, sinless life. He died on the cross for our sins, and on the third day, He rose to life so we could have salvation.

Grace Day

My grace is sufficient for you, for my power is made perfect in weakness.
2 Corinthians 12:9a

Week 4

What feels like so many moons ago, I, Bethany, taught preschool. I started my teaching career with the baby 2 1/2 year olds. I also taught 4's, but that's a story for another day. In my class, we had an afternoon tradition. Each day, one of my babies would choose a book for us to read before everybody started heading home. There was never a fight, really, unless it came to this one book. Certainly some of you have heard of it...it's a Sesame Street favorite, The Monster at the End of This Book.

Two of my baby boys, let's call them Travis and James, loved/hated this book. When James picked it, life was good, but if his best bud, Travis, picked it, look out world – a flood of tears and fears was a'comin'!

This particular day, Travis picked our book...and guess which one he grabbed? ou got that right! Monster time! James quickly scooted as close to me as humanly possible, covered his baby blues with his chubby little two-year-old hands and said, "Miss Beffany, pwwweasssseeeee don't read that book! There's a monster at the end of it!" I looked at him, a tad confused, and said, "James, we've read this book before! You know the ending as well as I do!" Convinced there was a monster, he sat, eyes shielded from the pages, as I read.

Well, if you've never read the book, Grover, our furry old friend, guides you through page after page of obstacles. As you read through the book, you have to be the good preschool teacher that we all know and love, who pretends to struggle to turn page after page because of the bricks or pipes or whatever other obstacle seems to be blocking your way to the next page.

Every time I glanced down, I'd see James, peeking ever so slightly through his tiny fingers. When he noticed that I was looking, he'd look away quickly. Finally, we reached the end of the book. Spoiler Alert: there's no monster! James popped up and said to me, "Miss Beffany, I toldddddd you there was no monster! It was just furry old Grover." I had to smile, "Silly me, James! Why was I so scared this whole time?"

To be honest, I think what scared my little friend wasn't so much the monster himself, but the idea of being trapped with the monster. I think we can relate. We sometimes feel trapped where we are. It's almost like we feel that God has asked us to "live" with a "monster"...our unwanted job feels monster-ish...our lack of a job feels monster-ish...our impossible boss feels monster-ish...the list goes on and on. What we fail to realize in our moments of fear is two-fold: #1: Our God is greater and more powerful than any "monster" in our path, and #2: God allows us to face monster-ish obstacles to strengthen us and grow us and pull us closer to Himself.

This week, let's uncover our baby blues and see if we can discover God's purpose for obstacles and monsters.

DAY 1
Grace Notes

I Got Saved

Grace Treasured

But God, being rich in mercy, because of the great love with which he loved us, even when we were dead in our trespasses, made us alive together with Christ — by grace you have been saved — and raised us up with him and seated us with him in the heavenly places in Christ Jesus.
Ephesians 2:4-6

Have you ever felt trapped or stuck in life, in your job, in your marriage? Or on a lighter note, teachers may feel trapped in the four walls of their classroom. Can we say #pottybreak? While Paul did not experience this kind of imprisonment, he certainly knew what it felt like to be in prison. This week while you are studying, keep in mind the areas where you feel trapped. We are praying that you realize the freedom you have in Christ.

Open your Bible and read Ephesians 3:1-6.

"For this reason I, Paul, a prisoner for Christ Jesus on behalf of you Gentiles - "

In green, circle what Paul calls himself.

When we say prison, don't think about a modern day prison. The Roman prison was much more intense. Let us explain.

Imagine...
A cave type dwelling with two levels. One level hanging from the top of the cave. One level lined the bottom. No bathrooms. Chains to bind hands and feet.

Can you imagine the stench? Can you imagine being on the bottom row when someone above you needed to relieve himself?

Paul was here. So was his scribe. It was bad enough that Paul had to be there, but imagine being his scribe who VOLUNTEERED to sit with Paul in these conditions and copy these God-breathed words. This person HAD to have known the importance and power of what Paul was writing.

This gives Philippians 4:4 a whole new meaning. Go read it and write it below. In case you are wondering...YES!...he was in prison while writing those words, too.

Go back and underline who Paul was in prison "on behalf of."

As we learned in chapters 1 and 2, Paul had been preaching to the Gentiles. The preaching of the Gospel was what landed Paul in prison on several occasions.

Before we go any further, read Ephesians 3:13. Paul wasn't seeking pity or freedom, but he realized that preaching the Gospel was for the benefit of the Gentiles.

Underline who Paul is a prisoner "for."

Paul realized that even though he was captured in a Roman prison, his imprisonment was for Christ Jesus.

So what does that even mean? How can you be a prisoner for Christ?

ROMAN PRISON	PRISONER FOR CHRIST
Paul is completely under the authority of the prison.	Paul is completely under the authority of Jesus Christ.
Paul cannot step outside of the boundaries of his captors.	Paul cannot step outside of the boundaries of his faith that been set by the Holy Spirit.
Paul is totally dependent upon the prison for all of his needs.	Paul is totally dependent upon the Lord for all of his needs.
Paul can do nothing that is outside the influence of the prison.	Paul can do nothing that is outside the influence of God.
The prison sees everything that Paul does.	The Lord sees everything that Paul does.
Disobedience results in immediate and thorough discipline.	Disobedience results in [...] thorough discipline from God.

*Carter, J.W. *Redemption: Faith Without Compromise*. 2011. 18 4 2017. <http://www.biblicaltheology.com/eph/49_03_01.html>.

Remember the situation that we asked you to think about today? The one that has you feeling imprisoned? Are you being a prisoner for Christ in the midst of that situation?

Let's put our names in the right side of that chart to understand what it means to be a prisoner for Christ.

_____ is completely under the authority of Jesus Christ.

_____ cannot step outside of the boundaries of her faith that been set by the Holy Spirit.

_____ is totally dependent upon the Lord for all of her needs.

_____ can do nothing that is outside the influence of God.

The Lord sees everything that _____ does.

Disobedience results in [...] thorough discipline from God.

Grace Point

Reflect on any areas of disobedience that have come from not submitting to the authority of Jesus Christ.

DAY 2

Have you ever asked God, "why me?" "why here?" "why now?" "why this?" We certainly have been at this place in our walks with God. In today's text, Paul seems to have similar thoughts on his mind.

Read Ephesians 3:7-13.

Look at verse 8. What seems to be his "why me?" statement? What does he call himself?

This is a good time for us to explore a little more history about our good friend, Paul. We feel like we can call him our friend now. Go to Acts 26 so we can listen in on Paul's retelling of his come-to-Jesus story. Read Acts 26:12-18.

So Paul was not his original name. His name was Saul, and he was known as a murderer of Christians. Until his conversion on the road to Damascus, his name was one that brought fear to many Christians. When Saul had his life-altering encounter, the Lord changed his name to Paul.

A little brain snack: Your name was your identity in Bible times. Parents chose their children's names based on the character they desired for them to exhibit. As a teacher, when we think of certain names, we ban them from our future children's name choices. You know what we mean. There are certain names that remind you of certain children that leave a very bad taste in your mouth. Saul would have been on the "banned names" list for every Christian. However, if you watch when the disciples and apostles chose to follow Jesus, He changed their names. Abram became Abraham. Sarai became Sarah. Saul became Paul. It's as though Jesus was saying, "You are no longer your old self. You have a new identity." (More on that next week in chapter 4.)

One thing is abundantly clear: Paul knew he was truly "the least of all the saints." To be quite blunt, he knew he had been a murderer of these people to whom he had been called to preach. However, his calling was clear.

In Acts 26:16, what does Paul say Jesus appointed him to do?

You see, Paul knew had Jesus not made him a minister of the Gospel, he never would have made himself a minister. He knew he wasn't worthy. He knew he, the least of all saints, needed grace upon grace to do what he had been called to do.

Perhaps this is how you are feeling in your "why me?" "why here?" "why now?" "why this?" situation. While this feeling applies to many situations, we can all relate it to our first year of teaching. We wonder: "Will my kids be where they need to be by the end of the year?" "Will I be able to reach all of my students' needs?" "Have I failed them?" "Do I *really* know what I'm doing?" "Am I going to damage them forever?"

Paul knew that what God called him to do, He would equip him to do. If you are a teacher, God will equip you to meet the needs of the students in your care. If you are a mom, God will equip you to raise and disciple the children with which God has entrusted you. If you are retired, God will equip you to minister and disciple those He places in your path.

Has there ever been a time when you have felt inadequate? Explain that time below or spend a few minutes thinking about it.

The feeling of inadequacy is a lie from Satan. Ephesians 3:12 holds a truth that will help us to defeat this lie. Write the verse below.

So we can have _____ and _____ with _____.

This truth is huge! When we feel inadequate, we can freely approach the One who called us, confident that He will not only listen to us, but will supply us with what we need to carry out what He has called us to do. That's God's grace!

Let's end today by listening to "Grace" by Laura Story.

DAY 3

Remember, on day one of this week, we said that Paul was writing this letter from prison. I think we all would agree that being in prison would be classified as a "worst day ever" experience. But we are about to see Paul do something that should make us go, "hmmmm."

Read Ephesians 3:14-19 to see what Paul is up to now.

What does verse 14 tell us he is doing? _____

That's right! Paul is praying even in the midst of his chains! Prayer is often a natural response in a crisis situation; however, usually it is prayer for rescue OUT of the situation. Paul wasn't praying to be rescued. He was praying for his friends in Ephesus yet again. Remember chapter 1? You see, even our worst sufferings shouldn't cause us to neglect praying for those to whom we have been called to minister. Our students. Our children. Our family. Our friends.

Let's take a look at what he's praying for the Ephesians this time.

Before we get too far...

A little brain snack: Notice Paul's posture. He "bow[ed] [his] knees" as he prayed. His bodily posture indicated his heart posture. He knew that God was God, and he was not and that meant Paul needed to show that he knew his position before God. We live in a "Jesus is my homeboy" culture, yet Jesus is not our "homeboy." We often think of Jesus as He is presented in the New Testament. He's loving and gracious and kind. Though that is 100% who He is, we sometimes forget He is also the God we see in the Old Testament. The God who turned a woman into a pillar of salt when she disobeyed. The God who opened the earth to swallow people whole when they sinned. The God who sent bears to devour people who mocked His servants. As Hebrews 13:8 reminds us, "[He] is the same yesterday, today, and forever," so He hasn't changed. The one thing – or person – that stands between us and the God of the Old Testament is Jesus Christ crucified in our place. This is why we should approach Him with reverence.

Okay, back to what Paul was praying. He prayed for 5 different things:

 Have you ever watched someone go through a trial - cancer, loss of job, loss of a loved one, chronic illness, bankruptcy - and wondered where they got their strength? The kind of strength Paul was talking about in Ephesians 3:16 is what sustains a Christian during these times. This strength is a strength that comes from within. It is a strength that taps into the power of your Savior, King Jesus.

 Look up Proverbs 4:23. As one beloved theologian said, "Where His Spirit dwells, there He swells." The more Jesus that we put into our hearts, the more Jesus will come out. Ever heard the saying, "Garbage in, garbage out?" This is the same idea: "Jesus in, Jesus out." Paul is praying that the Ephesians would be a people who overflow Jesus to everyone around them.

 Think of a tree. The health of a tree is determined by its roots. You cannot staple an orange onto an apple tree. The orange would rot and die because it's not connected to the tree's life source, the roots. The same is true with us. The stronger the roots, the stronger the tree, and the better the fruit. The more we spend time with Jesus, the stronger our roots become, and therefore, the more love we produce.

 Read Job 11:7-9. God's love cannot be measured. Remember how we said that there are things about God around which we cannot wrap our minds? His love is one of them. It's broader, longer, higher, and deeper than we can fathom. Look up one more passage: Psalm 139. Read it in a spirit of prayer, acknowledging that your Savior knows you from the inside out and loves you even still. As Corrie ten Boom says, "No matter how great our depths are, He is deeper still."

Don't throw a conniption fit! We know we left off number 5! Purposeful cliffhanger here. Contain yourself from skipping ahead to day 4. We know you want to look, but hold your horses. Until then...

Grace Point

Ask the Lord to show you who He wants you to be praying for right now. Use Paul's prayer as a model to spend a few minutes praying for them.

DAY 4

Okay...so who cheated? Did you skip ahead? We know someone did...because we would have at least glanced at it.

Just a little recap. We left Paul in the middle of his prayer for the Ephesians. Remember, he is praying from prison.

Below, we have given you blank numbers. Look back at yesterday's notes and write inside the numbers the 4 things that Paul prayed for the Ephesians.

Now, let's take a look at his final prayer for them. But first, go back and re-read Ephesians 3:4-21.

 Have you ever felt empty and tried to fill that emptiness with drugs, sex, alcohol, shopping, exercise, friendships, relationships, etc. only to feel empty again? It's because as it has been said, we all have a "God-shaped vacuum in [our] heart[s]" that can only be filled by God. Essentially, Paul was praying that the Ephesians would be full of God. He wanted them to want God above everything else.

Paul now closes his prayer by recognizing the power of the God he has been addressing. Read Ephesians 3:20-21 below.

"20Now to him who is able to do far more abundantly than all that we ask or think, according to the power at work within us, 21to him be glory in the church and in Christ Jesus throughout all generations, forever and ever. Amen."

On the next page, you will see a staircase. These verses seem to build a staircase that describes the power of God. Below, we have numbered each level of the staircase. Starting at the bottom, write on each step the level labeled below.

1able to do 2far more abundantly 3than all that we ask 4or think.

God's power is much greater than we can imagine. That same power, according to verse 20, is at work within you and me, too. This is the same power that turned water into wine. This is the same power that parted the Red Sea. This is the same power that caused Jonah to be swallowed up in the belly of a whale. This is the same power that healed the woman who bled for 12 years. This is the same power that gave Lazarus life. This is the same power that raised Jesus from the dead. That's some powerful power!

But let's pause for a second. This verse is sometimes taken out of context. God is not a genie in a bottle. Paul is NOT saying that whatever we ask for, we get. He IS saying that God will give us whatever we need in order to carry out the task He has given to us. Remember, our lives are for HIS glory, not our own glory. Everything that we do should be to further the Gospel. If it's not pointing to Jesus, it's not worth doing. Jesus at the center should always be our motto. When He's not at the center, life is off balance and needs an adjustment.

It's interesting to note that every time Paul prays, he prays that the Ephesians would know more about God. He doesn't pray for safety. He doesn't pray for blessings to overwhelm them.

He prays that they would know as much about God as humanly possible.
He prays that they would be filled with as much of God as humanly possible.
He prays that they would display God as much as humanly possible.

You hear the reason for his prayer in verse 21. It's for HIS glory..."throughout ALL generations, forever and ever. Amen."

A little brain snack: Ever wonder what that word "Amen" means? We seem to casually end every prayer with it, but most of us are clueless what we are saying. It's simple, really. It means "so be it" or "let it be so." So when Paul closes this prayer, he is essentially saying, "Lord, let it happen - all that I've prayed for these people - all that I've prayed about You receiving the glory - let it be so.

As you end today, we'd like you to settle in and listen to one of our FAVORITE songs right now. Can you tell we like music?? Get comfy because it's a little longer than some of our others, but we promise - it's gonna be SO worth it!

Israel Houghton, do yo' thang...

Grace Day

My grace is sufficient for you, for my power is made perfect in weakness.
2 Corinthians 12:9a

Week 5

I, Bonnie, am the worst kindergarten teacher in the world. Just kidding. However, after this day, I pretty much felt that way. Let me back up a bit...I normally wear contacts daily. On rare occasions, when my eyes hurt, I will wear my glasses. We were about halfway through the school year, and I decided on this particular day that I would wear my glasses.

If you have ever taught kindergarten, you know that some of your little friends can develop a crush on their teacher. #alwaysflattering This little friend, let's call him Max, had a crush on me. He would bring me flowers, draw me pictures, and had even previously proposed marriage.

As we began our day, I heard, "I like your glasses." "You look nice in your glasses, Miss Hunter." "I didn't know Miss Hunter wore glasses." I smiled and continued to teach. Meanwhile, my friend Max had snuck back to his cubby and dug in his backpack for a special treasure.

I looked up at my class of kindergarten students, and there sat Max, grinning and beaming with pride. Except, this time, Max had on glasses. MAX HAS GLASSES!?!?! I was confused and perplexed as to why this was the first time I had seen Max with glasses during the school year - we were in the third quarter of the school year, mind you. I asked Max where he had gotten his glasses. He simply replied that they had come from his bookbag. Fortunately, Max was a twin, and his twin brother, who also in my classroom, piped in and said, "YEAH! He has glasses! Our granny cleans his glasses every night for him!"

To say I was perplexed was an understatement. In the last 5 minutes, I had learned that one of my students wore glasses and needed to be wearing them every day to do his work. Not only did I learn that he needed them, but I learned that his poor grandmother was taking the glasses out of his backpack each night and carefully cleaning them and placing them back in his backpack. SMH. If you don't know texting acronyms, SMH stands for "shaking my head," which I was doing...very hard. Truly, I was shaking my head in shame. I felt awful that I didn't know that the poor baby had glasses and needed them to see...ummmm...his work. To my defense, his parents didn't realize he wasn't using them or that he had not told me that he needed them.

In the coming weeks, it seemed as though a light bulb came on for Max. He was reading better. His handwriting was 3 times neater. Poor baby couldn't see. He needed his glasses to open his eyes.

Max wasn't the only one who needed glass to help his eyes see more clearly. The Ephesians needed spiritual glasses to understand all that Paul was teaching them. This week, Paul's topics range from unity to putting off parts of the old nature. Some of us, exactly like the Ephesians - and Max - think we can see ourselves clearly. We don't really need our spiritual glasses. But if we're honest with ourselves, when we look through Jesus' eyes, we know we will find things from our old nature that we need to "put off." Just like Max improved in his schoolwork after he began faithfully wearing his glasses, we, too, will improve in our walk with Jesus when we commit to seeing ourselves through His eyes every day.

DAY 1
Grace Notes

Called Me Higher

Grace Treasured

So that in the coming ages he might show the immeasurable riches of his grace in kindness toward us in Christ Jesus.
Ephesians 2:7

We have reached the halfway mark though the book of Ephesians. Chapters 1-3 have focused on theology and doctrine while chapters 4-6 are going to be focused more on application.

We know that a kindergarten teacher has to do her job teaching the basics in order for a child to do well in later grades. If a teacher in a previous grade drops the ball, then the next teacher will see the holes in the development of the child. Each teacher has a special role and responsibility to shape each child's life.

Paul was a teacher as well. He knew that building blocks had to start with theology and doctrine before he could give the people of Ephesus practical application. This is like a child needing number sense before they can multiply and divide.

Most people enjoy chapters 4 through 6 more than chapters 1 through 3 because they have more practical information. This is much like our students who want to know why they need to learn something. However, practical application becomes nothing more than a legalistic checklist unless we know our theological and doctrinal building blocks first. We have to have the roots in order to have the fruits. A tree without deep roots is easily swayed.

Read Ephesians 4:1-7.

Vocabulary to Know

Theology: what you believe about God and why
Doctrine: a summary statement about a specific Biblical topic

Yet again, what does Paul call himself?

How does Paul urge the Ephesians to walk?

What does it mean to walk in a manner that is worthy of our calling? This means that we are enemies of sin, but friends of love, unity, purity, and holiness.

Paul's ultimate goal in this section was to teach the Ephesians how to maintain unity. In verses 2-3, Paul mentions 5 attributes that will help us achieve and maintain unity. List those 5 attributes below.

Let's define these attributes.

Bearing with one another in love: do not cease loving for any reason

Gentleness: unwilling to provoke others; not easily provoked or offended

Patience: slow to take revenge

Eager to maintain unity: To be quick to make peace

humility: opposite of pride, considering others before your own

Individually these ingredients are good. Eggs are good. Butter is certainly good....especially on fresh, flaky biscuit. Sugar is great in coffee. Flour can make some good pancakes. However, all of these together make something even better...yes, better than a butter biscuit.

Unity is much like baking. Many of the attributes can stand on their own and be quite good, but together they make a unity so "delicious" that non-believers can't help but wonder why we are so different. Our faith should set us apart. As we start removing ingredients, our cake falls apart. The same is true with unity. As we remove humility, gentleness fades. As we remove gentleness, patience dies. As we remove patience, love ceases. As we remove love, unity disappears.

Why was unity so important to Paul? Think about the Ephesians' culture.

Go back and read Ephesians 4:4-5. How many times is the word "one" repeated?

Yes, it was repeated 7 times. In the Bible, the number 7 is the number of perfection. This recipe for unity was perfection in Paul's eyes and, most importantly, in God's eyes. God's plan for His children is unity.

Unity was a priority for the Ephesians because it set them apart from their divisive culture. Their culture was a hot mess. Much like our culture today. Obtaining these attributes of unity would set them apart.

Grace Point

Spend a few moments listing reasons why unity is vital in your home, your classroom, your school, your relationships, your church, and your extended family.

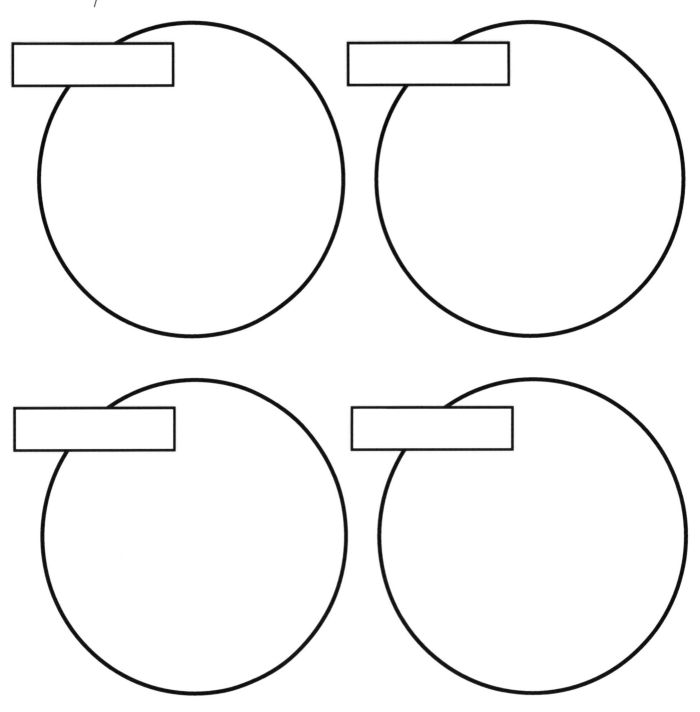

DAY 2

We left Paul yesterday reminding the Ephesians of the importance of unity. Another reason unity is important is...

¹⁴...so that we may no longer be children, tossed to and fro by the waves and carried about by every wind of doctrine, by human cunning, by craftiness in deceitful schemes.

Our job here is not to point any fingers or name any names; however, there are some popular Bible teachers in our culture right now that take Scripture out of context and lead you to believe something is a Biblical truth that is not. Paul knew that it was important for the Ephesians to understand doctrine and theology so that they would be rooted and grounded in truth and able to easily recognize false teaching.

We know that many of you come from different denominations of faith. Some may be Presbyterian. Some Baptist. Some Methodist. Some Catholic. Some Non-Denominational. However, we are still called to unity. As the saying goes, "...in essentials, unity; in non-essentials, liberty; in all things, love." Our essentials are what we studied in chapters 1 through 3: Jesus was born of a virgin. He lived a perfect, sinless life. He is fully God and fully man. He died on the cross and rose again on the third day. He is our only means of salvation. In these things, we must be unified. These essentials were what Paul was wanting the Ephesians to be grounded in so that they would detect when someone was preaching a different "gospel."

Go ahead and read Ephesians 4:14-16.

In the very beginning of verse 15, Paul tells the Ephesians how to speak to those who aren't teaching truth. They are to...

SPEAK THE TRUTH IN LOVE.

Let's talk classroom management for a minute. There are 3 classroom management styles:

Teacher #1: She is the "I love you so much I can't stand it!!!" teacher. The problem with this teacher is that there's SO much love that discipline and accountability take a back seat. In this classroom, kids feel like they can get away with anything.

Teacher #2: She is the "Wicked Witch of the West." There is NO grace in her classroom. Her kids fear her and walk on eggshells. This is the teacher who says that you can't smile before Christmas. The problem with this teacher is that due to the lack of love, a relationship is missing. Rules without relationship lead to rebellion.

Teacher #3: She is the "speak the truth IN love" teacher. Her kids know she loves them. Her classroom procedures are clear. Her expectations are high. She goes the extra mile to make sure that her children know they are well-loved, which earns her the ability to speak hard truths to them and hold their feet to the fire.

Teacher #3 sounds an awful lot like Jesus. He was first and foremost concerned with making sure people felt loved; however, He also spoke hard truths to them about their sin. This reminds us of the story of the Woman at the Well. Let's take a minute and read her story in John 4. When you're finished reading John 4:1-26, meet us back here.

Let's recap what you just read...

SOMEONE The Samaritan woman

WANTED living water — salvation

BUT Jesus reminded her of her 5 husbands and the man she was living with then

SO we are led to believe she repented of her sin

THEN Jesus revealed Himself as the Messiah she had been waiting to see.

Jesus didn't shy away from speaking the truth to this woman, but He also gave her the greatest gift of love by offering her Living Water. Sometimes we can be fearful about speaking truth to those that we love, but to love someone means that sometimes we have to speak difficult truths to rescue them from their sin. If this is done without love, then it becomes judgmental and harsh with a "holier-than-thou" attitude. If we choose just to love and ignore truth, then that's not really love at all.

Casting Crowns has a great way of reminding us of this truth through song. Take a moment to listen to their song, "Love You With the Truth."

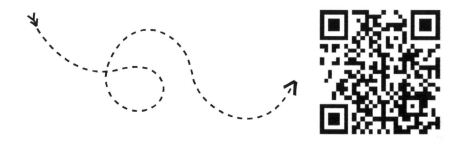

DAY 3

Read Ephesians 4:17-32.

Bonnie can remember her momma telling her often, "Bonnie, you are a Hunter, and you know what that means. You represent me and your daddy! Act like it." Essentially, this is what Paul was saying in these verses. Read Ephesians 4:20. Honestly, that verse makes both of us chuckle. We think you should write it.

It is almost is like he is saying, "I didn't raise you that way! You know better than that. You are a Christian, and you know what that means. You represent Jesus. Act like it."

In verse 22, Paul begins to remind the Ephesians what representing Jesus looks like. You can tell we are both 80's babies because his words remind us of the Karate Kid: "Wax on, wax off." Paul's version would say, "Put off, put on."

Put OFF. ➡ Put ON.

Put OFF	Put ON
YOUR OLD SELF ➡	YOUR NEW SELF
LYING ➡	TRUTH IN LOVE
SINFUL ANGER ➡	RIGHTEOUS ANGER
GIVING PLACE TO THE DEVIL ➡	GIVING PLACE TO THE SPIRIT
STEALING ➡	HONEST WORK
CORRUPT TALK ➡	GRACIOUS TALK
BITTERNESS, WRATH, ANGER, CLAMOR, AND SLANDER ➡	KINDNESS, TENDERHEARTEDNESS, AND FORGIVENESS

We are both very hands-on teachers. We like doing interactive activities in our classrooms. Yes, Bethany plans centers for her high school students. No lie. She don't play. I mean they play in the centers...but she doesn't mess around. So it is time for an interactive activity. Get out your sticky notes and your favorite pen. If you MUST have different colors...grab 'em!

We have provided boxes with things you should put off. Look back to the list we gave you on the previous page and find the "put on" item that matches the "put off" item in each box. Write the "put on" item on a sticky note and cover up the "put off" item.

YOUR OLD SELF

LYING

SINFUL ANGER

GIVING PLACE
TO THE DEVIL

STEALING	CORRUPT TALK

BITTERNESS, WRATH, ANGER, CLAMOR, AND SLANDER	

Grace Point

Spend a few moments reflecting on some areas in your life that you may need to "put off." Write one area down in the extra box above and cover it up with a sticky note of something that you need to "put on."

DAY 4

We are positive that you want us to go back and expound on the "put off" items from yesterday. Some of you may have even said, "What does that ONE even mean?" We can read your minds. We will spend today unpacking what we learned yesterday.

Yesterday, we had you cover up "put off" items with sticky notes. The whole reason behind that activity was to help you understand that the "put off" items are sins in our lives that are part of our old nature. Jesus' blood covered those sins on the cross just as the sticky notes covered the sin words.

The act of "putting on" is like getting dressed every day. You wouldn't go outside without clothes. At least we hope not. If we don't intentionally "put on" these fruits of the Spirit daily, then the "put offs" come back. They are still there. They are covered, but they are not gone. Salvation doesn't mean that we are no longer sinners. We are still sinners who are tempted to sin daily. Therefore, we must repent and turn away and ask the Holy Spirit to help us. The big difference is that our sin was covered and paid for by Jesus on the cross in our place.

Let's take a closer look at the "put offs" and "put ons." Go back and re-read Ephesians 4:17-32.

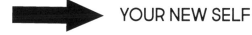

Your old self is the sinful nature with which you were born. Your new self is your new nature in Christ.

If I, Bonnie, walked down the hall and told my first grade teacher neighbor, "My kindergarten students have THE best handwriting!" She would naturally assume that I taught them handwriting. The next school year, she would expect her new group of students to have fantastic handwriting. When she saw that Billy could not correctly form the letter A, she would know that I had lied. You see, lies don't gain you benefit in the long run; they hurt you and those around you. We are back at Paul's command to "speak the truth in love."

SINFUL ANGER  RIGHTEOUS ANGER

Write Ephesians 4:26 below.

In red, underline the first two words. In pink, circle the conjunction. In red, underline the second command that follows the conjunction.

Did that statement make you scratch your head and go, "huh??" We've always been taught that anger is a sin. But that's NOT what Paul is saying. Anger, in certain situations, is permissible...especially in cases of injustice or anything that opposes God or His nature.

Examples: I can be righteously angry about ISIS fighters killing innocent Christians. I cannot be righteously angry about my husband leaving dirty dishes everywhere. I can be righteously angry about young girls being sold into sex trafficking. I cannot be righteously angry about having to fill in on someone's duty at school.

GIVING PLACE TO THE DEVIL  GIVING PLACE TO THE SPIRIT

Giving place to the devil is like leaving the door cracked where he can slide his slimy, sinful self right in and tempt you to fall into all sorts of his traps. Falling into one of these traps is NOT permission to blame him for your sin. When we repeatedly blame Satan for our choices, we give him waaaaaaaaayyyyyy too much credit! Remember, Satan is NOT all-knowing. He may tempt you, but he has no way of knowing what decision you're going to make.

Example: When I neglect to have time alone in my Bible, I am more tempted to have a bad attitude. However, when I've spent time alone with Jesus, my attitude will reflect Him as it should.

STEALING  HONEST WORK

All English teachers know the struggle of teaching plagiarism to their students. To students, copying someone else's work is easy and somewhat genius because "my teacher won't know it's not mine!" To teachers, copying someone else's work cripples students because they lose the value of learning to turn their thoughts into words. Paul knew that while stealing might seem easier and immediately beneficial, in the long run, it robbed them of learning that hard work pays off.

Can you think of a time where you know that honest work paid off for you? Reflect on that time or write about it below.

CORRUPT TALK ➡ GRACIOUS TALK

Have you ever felt like you stuck your foot in your mouth? I, Bonnie, have to remind myself to stay in my lane. Oftentimes, my mouth can get me in trouble because I choose to react to things instead of respond.

What is the difference between reacting to something and responding to something?

Corrupt talk is tearing someone down. It's not giving them grace. It's talking about the teacher down the hall and how she doesn't do things the way you think she should. It's making sarcastic remarks. Sarcasm finds its bite in the bitterness in our hearts. (Side note: Both of us are VERY sarcastic in nature! But when sarcasm is used to speak what you really think cloaked with "humor," then it's sin.)

Gracious talk is building someone up. It's giving LOTS of grace. It's complimenting the teacher down the hall, letting her know what you think she does well.   It's encouraging. It's knowing when to speak and when to listen. As our pastor said, "To listen to someone is to love them."

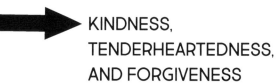

BITTERNESS, WRATH, ANGER, CLAMOR, AND SLANDER ➡ KINDNESS, TENDERHEARTEDNESS, AND FORGIVENESS

Bitterness, wrath, and anger are inward, violent resentments toward others. Clamor and slander are outward words and threats. Basically, clamor and slander are the outward expressions of bitterness, wrath, and anger.

Kindness is an outpouring of love that's in our hearts. To be tenderhearted means you are able to put yourself in another person's shoes and sympathize with them and show compassion to them.

In kindergarten, it is a common thing to see several kindergarteners rush to the aid of someone who has fallen. They will express genuine concern and want to help. If someone spills crayons on the floor, it wouldn't be surprising if five friends got up and helped pick up the crayons. Maybe that's why God said we should have child-like faith...because...

In high school, it is a common thing to see several fingers pointed at someone who has fallen as they laugh rather than help. Not only do they often not help, but you can watch many pull out their phones to video and post the fall on social media. If someone spilled something on the floor, it wouldn't be surprising if students stayed in their seats while they ignored the help that was needed.

Grace Point

One of our favorite theologians reminds us that we are to "provoke one another's graces, not passions." In other words, we are to look for ways to bring out the best sides of those around us, not their worst sides. Brainstorm specific ways that you can bring out someone's best side. Choose someone who is close to you. If you're struggling, ask the Lord to help you. Remember, it's always okay to walk away from your Bible study for a bit and come back as He brings the ideas to your mind.

Grace Day

My grace is sufficient for you, for my power is made perfect in weakness.

2 Corinthians 12:9a

Week 6

Have you ever noticed how imitating adults is almost a game to kids?

I, Bonnie, love teaching kindergarten. Kinders are amazing imitators. They watch what other kids do, and they follow suit. Not only do they watch kids, they watch the adults around them as well. Sometimes I hear my kindergarten students say something like, "This table is atrocious!" and I know they have been in my classroom too long. Haha. They have heard me say that many times before, and if I'm honest, I can hear my mother saying that, too. I imitated her; they imitate me.

Kinders aren't the only great imitators. Older elementary students jump on that bandwagon, too. Our fifth graders this year have become obsessed with Rubik's cubes. It started when a child moved to our school during the middle of the year. He had the talent of figuring out the Rubik's cube in 30 seconds. All of the other fifth graders were amazed. Quite frankly, the teachers on our hall were as well. Over the following weeks, we noticed that our fifth grade students started bringing in Rubik's cubes, and our new student was teaching them how to solve the puzzle. It slowly trickled down to fourth grade, and before the end of the school year, I noticed a few third graders bringing in Rubik's cubes. Fourth grade imitated fifth grade; third grade imitated fourth grade.

You know, come to think of it, adults are pretty great imitators, too. Our teachers started the school year competing with our Fitbit bands. One Fitbit competitor led to another, and soon, a great majority of teachers were competing for the top spot in our weekly competition. We are pretty competitive and try to sneak in extra steps. Students quickly got into the weekly competition. They would cheer if their teacher was in the lead. We have a first grade teacher who is competitive, and it overflowed to her classroom. The kids loved it. Soon, we noticed kids wearing the happy meal toy that was a step counter. We heard of kids asking for Fitbits over Christmas. Our older elementary kids started using their parents' old Fitbits and asking us to be friends with them through the Fitbit app. Our step count became a topic of conversation between the teachers and the students. Teachers imitated teachers; then, students imitated teachers.

Maybe it is just our school. Maybe we simply have a group of kids who are imitators. On second thought, I don't think it is just us. Kids watch adults. They watch their parents, and they certainly watch their teachers. During the school year, a child spends more waking hours with their teacher than they spend with their parents. This should give us pause. If our actions don't line up with our words, be sure, they will point them out or act them out for us - and others - to see.

Paul opens chapter 5 of Ephesians with this statement: "...be imitators of God, as beloved children." You see, the very best way that a child imitates his or her parents is through actions. Paul is calling the Ephesians, and you and me, to imitate the love and grace of their Heavenly Father. Join us as we take a closer look at how to imitate the One who is full of love and grace and mercy.

DAY 1
Grace Notes

Slow Fade

Grace Treasured

For by grace you have been saved through faith. And this is not your own doing; it is the gift of God, not a result of works, so that no one may boast.
Ephesians 2:8-9

Just like our song of the week from Casting Crowns, sin is a slow fade. Often sin creeps into our hearts and lives. You don't just wake up one day and walk off the cliff. The climb to the top of that mountain has been slow step by slow step. Oftentimes, we draw a line in the sand of where we will not go. However, our little pedicured toes will tip-toe right up to that line. We are FINE as long as we don't cross that line. However, straddling that line is proof of a heart issue. We begin to challenge the "line" instead of fleeing the line.

Paul is reminding the Ephesians in chapter 5 that they are to be set apart. The center of their culture, remember, was a temple dedicated to a fertility goddess. Prostitution was the norm. Sexual immorality was standard. Sounds a bit like our culture, doesn't it? Okay…maybe minus the temple part.

Why don't you go ahead and read Ephesians 5:1-21.

With such a worldly culture surrounding them, it would have been super easy for the Ephesians to imitate the culture rather than their Heavenly Father. Paul doesn't want them confused and wondering what it looks like to imitate God, so he spends some time in chapter 5 giving them a very clear picture of what it does NOT look like and what it DOES look like.

As we explore these verses, may we keep in mind that Paul just taught them that truth must be spoken, but in love. Paul will be blunt. Truth is sometimes blunt. If my (Bethany) great niece, Zoey, was about to toddle into a busy intersection, it wouldn't be loving of me to let her go or even to calmly say, "Baby girl, come back here." No! I would scream at the top of my lungs, "ZOEY, NOOOOO!!" Even if it startled her, even if it brought tears to her sweet little eyes, it would be the most loving thing to do to save her life.

Paul is concerned with saving the Ephesians' souls. He will speak truth, hard truth, but they know he loves them.

Go through Ephesians 5:3-19 and pull out characteristics of an imitator of the world vs. an imitator of God. Write them on the girls. You will find 9 total for each. It is OKAY if you don't get all of them! Don't stress. Just find as many as you can.

No matter how many you found in the passage, we are sure that you can see a MASSIVE difference between an imitator of the world and an imitator of Christ. Tomorrow, we will dive more in-depth into these characteristics.

Grace Point

Take a moment to compare your life and see which one you are imitating more right now: the world or Jesus. Ask the Holy Spirit to reveal areas in your life where you need to imitate Him more than the culture around you.

DAY 2

Yesterday, we had you pull out some characteristics that Paul mentions in Ephesians 5 that help us to distinguish between someone who is imitating the world and someone who is imitating God. Why don't you re-read Ephesians 5:1-21 and meet us back here so we can take a closer look at some of those characteristics.

When teaching a difficult concept, a good teacher knows to present as many sides as possible to help students understand.

Grammar Nerd Alert: For example, when I, Bethany, teach verbals, I know I can't just demonstrate what a gerund, participle, or infinitive IS; I also need to show them what they are NOT, so that they can begin to distinguish between a verb and verbal.

The Elementary Side: For example, when I, Bonnie, teach kinders how to read a book, I show them that you read with excitement, not like a robot.

Paul, as a teacher, did just that in this section of Scripture. He knew that sometimes seeing both the worldly side and the godly side would help the Ephesians begin to recognize areas they needed to look a little more like Christ and a little less like their melting pot culture.

For our OCD peeps (like both of us) who want to go back and fix or add to your girls from yesterday, here's a list of the characteristics Paul mentions:

WORLD

1. Sexual immorality
2. Impurity
3. Covetousness
4. Filthiness
5. Foolish Talk
6. Crude Joking
7. Unfruitful Works of Darkness
8. Foolishness
9. Drunkenness

CHRISTIAN

1. Thanksgiving
2. Walk as Children of Light
3. Discern What is Pleasing to the Lord
4. Expose Unfruitful Works
5. Walk as Wise
6. Make the Best Use of Time
7. Understand What the Will of the Lord Is
8. Filled With the Spirit
9. Sing to the Lord

Some of these are self-explanatory, but some could use some clarification. Let's look at a few of them.

Covetousness. In verse 5, Paul mentions covetousness, or idolatry, as a trait of a world imitator. It's easy to brush this one off as most of us probably don't have statues around us.   However, covetousness is truly referring to putting anything in God's spot and wanting more and more and more of it. TV shows. Netflix. Relationships. Overworking. Dollar Tree. Notice that he follows this by saying these people "[have] no inheritance in the kingdom of Christ." This is a HUGE deal to God. He doesn't share His spot in our lives with anyone or anything else. We certainly love TV, Netflix, Dollar Tree, etc., but the moment that these things become bigger to us than God, something is wrong.   If something is more important to us than spending time with Him, we need to stop and re-evaluate because that is a sign we are imitating the world.

Unfruitful Works of Darkness.   Think of a tree again.   An apple tree that is unfruitful — produces no apples - is pointless. Unfruitful works have no point. They are wasting time and space. The fact that these works are done in darkness points also to their sinfulness. Paul goes on to say that as Christ followers, we should be exposing these deeds, not participating in them.

Drunkenness.   This is a touchy subject; however, this is OUR interpretation. The positive command in verse 18 is to "be filled with the Spirit." Being filled with the Spirit means that the Holy Spirit has total control of our hearts and lives. In a nutshell, it's Jesus being in control of my life. He is what I think about, sing about, and talk about. More about that tomorrow.   Paul's negative command here is "not [to] get drunk with wine." Notice it does NOT say not to be filled with wine. It says not to be **drunk** with wine. The definition of "drunk" would be to give up control. Paul is saying that the moment alcohol takes control of you, you are no longer in control and neither is the Holy Spirit. In Ephesus, it was common for them to have huge parties to celebrate their gods. Drunkenness was expected. Remember, Paul's purpose was to remind them they were to be set apart from their culture.

Discern What Is Pleasing to the Lord.   How do we know what pleases the Lord?   It's common to hear people say, "The Lord told me to _____ (fill in the blank)." The blank often does not match with Scripture.   The Lord never tells us to do anything that Scripture doesn't support. Pleasing the Lord is following and obeying what He has given to us in Scripture.

Understand What the Will of the Lord Is.   The will of the Lord is not a huge, hidden secret. His will is made known to us in His Word.   His ultimate will is that His Name would be made known. If you're unsure if something is God's will, ask yourself, "Will this make His name great?"

We know we've done a LOT of talking, so it's your turn.   Go to Psalm 1 in your Bible. Read the Psalm.

There's a progression happening in verse 1. Record the 3 verbs below.

Now look in verse 2. Where should our delight be found?

What does the godly person meditate on day and night?

Paul was explaining to the Ephesians how to walk as imitators of Christ. The Psalmist and Paul both knew that the slippery slope to sin was slow. As we see in Psalm 1:1, you begin by **walking** in the wrong place. Then you move to **standing** in the wrong place. Finally, you **sit** in the wrong place. Remind you of the pig wallowing in the mud again? Yep, us too. Paul and the Psalmist also knew that delighting in God's Word would help us to be imitators of Christ instead of imitators of the world. Paul was saying, "Walk this way."

DAY 3

Let's start today by re-reading Ephesians 5:1-2. Write verse 2 below.

Underline how we are to walk in the verse you wrote above.

Love is to be the defining characteristic of Christians because it is the defining characteristic of our Father. Remember, we are to be imitators of Him; that's Paul's main point in chapter 5.

Yesterday, Paul described the difference between an imitator of the world and an imitator of Christ. One of the characteristics of a Christ imitator was one who was filled with the Spirit. Let's get grammar-y for a minute…

In verse 18 of chapter 5, Paul gives the command to "be filled with the Spirit." If you continue reading, he then uses 5 participle phrases in verses 19-21 to help us understand what being filled with the Spirit looks like.

A little brain snack: In grammar, participles are verb words that have a suffix attached and act as an adjective. For example, if I say, "I am running." Running is a participle because run (verb) + -ing (suffix) = describes (adjective) the subject, I. Another example: Burnt toast is gross. Burnt is a participle here because burn (verb) + -t (suffix) = adjective describing toast (noun).

So let's look at how Paul has defined being filled with the Spirit (participles are bolded):
   1) **addressing** one another
   2) **singing** and **making** melody…
   3) **giving** thanks always
   4) **submitting** to one another

What does number 4 say that we should do to one another?

This word sometimes gets a bad rap. If this word has had a bad rap for you in the past, please stick with us - don't skip over this part. This message is for you, and we promise it is filled with a deep love from your Heavenly Father.

Whenever we say the word "submission" over the next two days, remember this definition:

submission: voluntarily yielding in love

In Ephesians 5:21, we learn that everyone should be submitting to one another. This is known as mutual submission. We need to understand mutual submission before we can understand submission in the context of marriage, which is what most of us think about when we hear the word submission. Let's look to Scripture for a couple of examples of mutual submission.

Philippians 2:3
How are we to treat others?

Philippians 2:5
Why do we treat others as more significant than ourselves?

Luke 22:26
Even leaders are called to do what?

Matthew 20:28
What were two of the reasons Jesus came?

Mutual submission is a way that we imitate Christ. He came to serve and SUBMITTED to the will of God the Father. Nobody took His life. Jesus willingly gave it. Essentially, this form of submission is considering someone else's needs above your own. It is voluntarily yielding in love.

submission: voluntarily yielding in love

Submission is NOT:
- a form of slavery.
- devaluing someone's opinion.
- being a doormat.
- being subject to physical or verbal or emotional abuse.
- belittling someone.
- a way to take away equality.

Submission IS:
- paying full attention to your boss during a staff meeting.
- taking someone's duty when you see they are overwhelmed.
- biting your tongue.
- responding to someone with love.
- putting yourself in someone else's shoes before speaking or acting.
- choosing to respond instead of react.

Grace Point

Today's grace point is a two part-er.

Part 1: Think of ways that you can be mutually submissive to someone in your life. If you are married, this is not your husband. We get to talk about him tomorrow. :-)

Part 2: Take a moment and ask God to prepare your heart for Bible study tomorrow. Particularly if you have ever been hurt by the idea of submission in the past, ask the Lord to soften your heart and open your ears to hear the truth about what HE had in mind for godly submission.

DAY 4

It's here. Today is the day for the "s" word. We treat this word like a curse word in the Christian world. Unfortunately, submission is misunderstood and mistreated by many in the church. That was not God's idea for submission. Submission is rooted in love. What did we say was the definition of submission yesterday?

Go back and read Ephesians 5:21-33. These verses are split into two parts: wives and husbands.

Many people will misinterpret this passage and apply mutual submission to the marriage relationship. It is important to understand mutual submission in order to fully understand marital submission; however, we know that the marriage relationship is not meant to be a place of mutual submission because Paul continues to describe three different relationships where mutual submission is not possible because of God's original and beautiful design.

Wives

We think that it is important for you to write Ephesians 5:22. Do that here.

Circle to whom wives are to submit.

Notice that the verse says "your own husbands." It does NOT say submit to every man walking down the street.

Underline the last four words of verse 22. Why are you submitting to your husband?

You are submitting to your husband because you love the Lord. NO OTHER REASON. It is not because he deserves it. It is not because he has done anything to earn it. IT IS BECAUSE you love the Lord. Period. End of Story.

Fill in the blank for verse 24 below.

> "²⁴Now as the church submits to Christ, so also wives should submit _____
>
> _____ to their husbands."

Jesus is painting a beautiful picture that compares the relationship between a husband and wife to the relationship between Christ and the Church. When He refers to the Church, He is referring to you and me - Christians, who are following Jesus.

The beginning of verse 24 reminds us that it is the Church's job to submit to Christ. Jesus is the One who has ultimate authority over the Church. We, the Church, are to submit to Him. We aren't to fight Him. We aren't to try to twist His arm. We aren't to nag Him. We are to submit, to yield in love, because He first loved us and gave Himself for us.

In the same way, Paul says wives should submit to their husbands in EVERYTHING. This doesn't mean the husband will always make the perfect choice. Humans aren't perfect. This doesn't mean the husband shouldn't listen to or consult his wife prior to making a decision. Women and men alike are made in God's image and have valuable insight. Paul's bottom line, however, is that the responsibility of authority rests on the shoulders of the husband, not the wife.

We hope that you aren't cringing. But if you are, HANG WITH US! Don't stop! We promise that by the end of this day, you will see a more beautiful picture of submission.

Husbands

If you're a math teacher, you're going to like this...there are 3 verses devoted to wives. There are 9 verses devoted to husbands. Bethany teaches English, and Bonnie teaches kindergarteners how to count every day — we both know that 9 is more than 3. In fact, it's 3 times more than 3! That's on purpose! God's Word is without error.

Look at verse 25. What is the very first command to husbands?

Now, in the same verse, how are husbands to love their wives?

When submission is carried out biblically, the husband's FIRST concern should be that EVERYTHING he does is demonstrating the same sacrificial love to his wife as Christ demonstrated to the church.

Read verse 28. How does Paul say that husbands are to love their wives in this verse?

In other words, husbands are to put their wives' needs before their own.

We hope you are beginning to see that submission practiced the way God designed it and the way Paul is describing it is truly beautiful.

We'd like you write one more verse today. Look at verse 33 of chapter 5 and record it below.

Put hearts around what husbands are to do and what wives are to do.

These two little words can get husbands and wives into a crazy cycle. When a husband feels disrespected, he's not going to be loving toward his wife. When a wife feels unloved, she is not going to be respectful toward her husband. We know men need respect and women need love, so somebody somewhere is going to have to stop the cycle.

Let's end today by looking at what submission IS and is NOT in the context of marriage.

Submission is NOT your husband:

- demanding that dinner be on the table when he gets home.
- taking away your voice.
- abusing you physically, verbally, or emotionally.
- taking advantage of you.
- demanding his way or the highway.

Submission IS you:

- desiring to take care of your husband's needs.
- listening to your husband.
- biting your tongue.
- allowing your husband to lead your family.
- praying for your husband.

Grace Point

If you're married, spend a few moments asking God how to best be submissive to your husband.

If you're single, spend a few moments praying for your future husband and/or asking God to help you to be submissive to Him.

Grace Day

My grace is sufficient for you, for my power is made perfect in weakness.
2 Corinthians 12:9a

Week 7

We don't know if you have ever witnessed a chick hatching, but it is one of the most amazing, yet somewhat scary and unpredictable experiences. Bonnie hatched chicks in her classroom toward the end of the year. We watched with baited breath to see how many of her 10 eggs would hatch. Twenty-one days is a loooooonnnnngggg time to wait, not just for kindergarteners, but for us, too!

One day before the actual hatch day, a tiny little pip appeared. We watched as a teeny-tiny little chick began to pop through the shell. The more this little baby started poking through, the more we became concerned. Bonnie had observed almost an entire day where the tiny chick had tried and tried to shed that shell, but it just wasn't happening. That same afternoon, the family who had brought in the eggs had come to see how the chicks were doing. The mom showed concern that more than half of the shell was still attached. Bonnie eventually sought help from the Facebook world. Some people begged her to help the precious, struggling baby; some people warned to let him come on his own.

Bonnie decided the poor little baby had experienced enough stress for the day - almost 12 hours of hatching is enough to kill anyone! After consulting 500+ people live on Facebook, she began to slowly and oh-so-carefully peel his shell away. We began to see that he, indeed, was stuck to his shell. The poor little thing looked SO exhausted. He was breathing hard, and we watched as little body went up and down and up and down over and over as he lay sleepily on the grates of the incubator.

Unsure if we should, we decided to leave him overnight to rest his worn-out little self. Praying we made the right decision to help him, we continued on with our night. We began to research whether or not you should help a chick hatch, and everything we read said nooooo!! Our hearts were literally heavy, thinking we were surely going to find a dead little chick in the incubator the next morning. No lie - we prayed for his tiny little body to bounce back; we knew it would be a miracle if he lived.

The next morning, we swiftly, yet slowly, walked into Bonnie's classroom. No chirping. No sounds at all. But lo and behold when we went over to the incubator, we peeked in to see, not one, but two little chicks. One popped up and started chirping at us immediately - that was Fuzzy Wuzzy. The other sat pretty still, but he was still live as live could be. About a quarter of his shell was still attached, so his "walk" was more of a hobble, but he made it! Little Pip...little now sassy-pants Pip was alive and well.

You see, during our research, we discovered one main reason you aren't supposed to help chicks hatch: the struggle makes them stronger. Is it just us, or does that strike you as a life lesson? Yep, that's what we thought.

There are times in our lives when we really want to help someone through a trial, but if we do, we cripple them more than help them. Let us be more specific - our research told us that typically when a chick is helped out of his shell, he dies. Something in us dies, too, when we are rescued rather than learning to fight. The same is true for us, too. Sometimes the best thing people can do for us is to let us fight. Help or rescue that comes too soon can cripple us. If you've ever wondered why your Heavenly Father doesn't always swoop in and rescue you, this is why. He knows what doesn't kill you, truly makes you stronger. The fight builds muscle. The fight builds faith.

However, in the fight, we need protection. Little Pip's shell was his protection. All his nutrients were tucked away in the eggshell-thin (pun totally intended haha) shelter that covered his little furry body. Removing it would cause him to miss gaining the very nutrients he needed to survive, which is why so many warned that it shouldn't be removed prematurely. The same is true with us. We have armor we are supposed to put on daily. If we pull off that armor before a battle is done, we lose what we need to survive.

Now, little sassy pants survived, but that isn't always so. He came out sassier than ever...in fact, he quite annoyed his incubator pal, Fuzzy Wuzzy. We're sure we aren't the only ones who have been rescued when perhaps we should've been left to fight.

This week, we are diving into one of Paul's most well-known passages about the Armor of God. Join us as we learn how vital that armor is to our daily fight for spiritual life.

DAY 1
Grace Notes

Your Grace Finds Me

Grace Treasured

For we are his workmanship, created in Christ Jesus for good works, which God prepared beforehand, that
we should walk in them.
Ephesians 2:10

First things first y'all - this is our last week together. Sad face. Don't cry. We already cried a few minutes ago...and more tears to come, we know.

Last week, we discussed the beauty of submission. We focused first on mutual submission and then moved to submission in marriage. Remember, we said that Paul described 3 different relationships where mutual submission was not possible based on God's design. Marriage was the first one, and we will take a look at the other two today.

Go ahead and read Ephesians 6:1-9.

What relationship do verses 1-4 discuss?

What relationship do verses 5-9 discuss?

It is easy to see how mutual submission would not work in either of these relationships. Children should submit to their parents, but parents should not submit to their children. Bondservants should submit to their masters, but masters should not submit to their bondservants.

Let's go ahead and take a peek at what Paul tells children their responsibility is. In verse 1, what does Paul tell children they are to do?

Paul's reason for telling children to obey makes us chuckle a bit because we hear a little whiny voice asking, "Whyyyyyyyyyyy????" We know you can hear the voice too. And what would our parents have said to us? "Because I said so!" Paul gives a similar response. It's a no if's, and's, or but's kind of response. Record his response from the end of verse 1 below:

Children are to obey because _____ _____ _____.

Kind of like wives are called to submit to their husbands because they love the Lord, Paul says children are to obey their parents because it's the right thing to do. In other words, "Because the Lord said so!"

If you continue to read into verse 2, you might pause because it seems a bit redundant. What is Paul's command to children in this verse?

While these two commands may sound similar, they have different meaning in the original language. Obey literally means to come under the authority of your parents — to submit to them. Honor means to esteem your parents as dear and value their opinions and wisdom. Typically, as you grow older, you shift more from obey to honor.

Let's look at the next relationship that Paul mentions: bondservants and masters.

Both of us have an ESV Bible. Bonnie's Bible uses the term "slaves" here. Bethany's Bible uses the term "bondservant." The Greek translation of this word is bondservant. A bondservant was someone who had been released from slavery but had chosen to remain with his or her master voluntarily.   This relationship compares most to our workplaces. From this point on, we will focus on the employee vs. employer relationship.

Re-read Ephesians 6:6. Who are we truly serving?

Both of us are people pleasers to the max. We can't stand having someone upset with us. It eats us alive. However, Paul points out that people-pleasing is not the goal. The goal is to serve Christ in the way we serve our employers.

How can we serve Christ as teachers?

Serving Christ as a teacher means doing your work for the Lord. Even if you're not in the grade level you want, even if you have the most hellacious class, even if your boss is a dictator, you choose to teach, providing the best educational experience you can for each and every student in your classroom. Even Billy.

submission: voluntarily yielding in love

DAY 2

Just as we are closing out our time together, Paul's letter to the Ephesians is coming to its close.   He had to feel some heartache, yet some "teacher pride," as he was preparing to send his precious students of the Word into the world. I can see him sitting in his prison cell, hand on chin, pen still in hand, "This one's gotta end strong...ah! armor! They need their armor to fight in this crazy, crooked, God-starved world. It's the only way I've survived."

Friends, you and I need that armor, too. This is one of my (Bethany) all time favorite passages in Scripture. I think it's perhaps so often taught that we breeze right over it. Please don't. These are Paul's final words. I know you'd listen to a good friend's final words. So lean in. Listen closely. Glean all you can.

Go ahead and read Ephesians 6:10-20.

First and foremost, before an army heads out to the battlefield, they need to know who they are fighting. Look at verse 12.

With whom do we wrestle?
   1.
   2.
   3.
   4.

All too often, we act as though the flesh and blood in front of us is our enemy.   Our boss. Our husband. Our friend. Our students. They are NOT the enemy. We attack them when truly, we should be suiting up and heading out to do battle with the real enemy, the one who plots and schemes against us. The devil.

WE THINK YOU SHOULD: If you have not yet watched the movie War Room, we think it would be fitting for this part of our study. It would be a fun family activity as well. You can find this movie at any Christian bookstore, or you can order it on Amazon.

On the next page, you will find the cutest little soldier. Using verses 14-17, label the 6 pieces of armor. There's technically a 7th "piece" of armor, but more on that later.

Take a moment to read the history of each piece of armor and how it applies to our walk with the Lord. As each topic is covered, color that piece of armor on our solider.

history

biblical application

The belt was one of the most central and important parts of the armor and had 2 main jobs. It was used to support the weight of the breastplate, which could be 50-60 pounds. It was also used to hold up soldiers' robes so it wouldn't trip them as they ran on the battlefield. They would gather the material from their ankle-length cloak and tuck it into their belt so that they had freedom to run quickly.

belt of truth

Knowing truth is vital. Paul began Ephesians, making sure that the people of Ephesus knew the truth about who they were and Whose they were. Without knowing the truth about Jesus and what He did for us on the cross, we would be left to carry the weight of our sin and left trying to earn our own righteousness. Truth also frees us up from lies that we believe about ourselves so that we can focus on what God has called us to do.

The breastplate was used to protect the most vital organ of the body: the heart. It was made out of metal, which could shield not only from sword stabs, but also the fiery darts, which we will discuss tomorrow.

breastplate of righteousness

Jesus' death on the cross allowed us to be viewed as righteous in the Father's eyes. The Bible says that our best attempts at being righteous are like filthy rags. Just as the breastplate protected the soldier's heart, thereby making the difference between life and death, Jesus' righteousness credited to us makes the difference between eternal life and eternal damnation.

A soldier's shoes were almost like cleats. The nails that were attached to the bottom helped them to "dig their heels" into the ground so they would not stumble on the hilly, rocky terrain. They also were strapped above their ankles, which gave the soldier even more stability and support.

shoes of peace

Paul spent a good portion of Ephesians focused on the importance of unity. The shoes of the Gospel of peace get their name from the fact that the greatest peace came when Jesus died on the cross to give us unity with the Father. When we put on the shoes of peace, we bring unity with us wherever we go. No matter how "rocky" the terrain around us gets, we can dig our heels in and stand firm, knowing we have full access to the Father through Jesus.

DAY 3

Yesterday, we started looking at the pieces of armor in Ephesians 6:10-20. Go ahead and re-read those verses.

What were the most interesting things you discovered about the 3 pieces of armor we've already discussed?

belt of truth

breastplate of righteousness

shoes of peace

Let's continue looking at the last 4 pieces of armor.

Take a moment to read the history of each piece of armor and how this applies to our walk with the Lord. As each topic is covered, color that piece of armor on our solider.

history

The shield that Paul is referencing here was quite large. It was about 2 feet by 4 feet and was covered in canvas and leather and had an iron center. This shield was quite heavy as I'm sure you can imagine. However, this shield is what blocked darts from the enemy. Fiery darts, which were literally dipped in tar and lit on fire, were easily stopped with this iron-centered shield. If soldiers got in a position where they couldn't defend themselves on their own, they would huddle in a circle and put their shields together, forming almost a "turtle shell" that would protect them from all sides.

shield of faith

biblical application

Faith is vital to the Christian life. James says that "faith without works is dead." When we don't act on faith, we are basically saying we don't believe God is Who He says He is or can do what He says He can do. When we do act in faith, it affirms that we believe Him. Acting in faith often stops the enemy from taunting us because he realizes we know God is real. However, there are times when our faith is weak, and we need our fellow brothers and sisters in Christ to come alongside us and remind us that God is Who He says He is and will do what He said He would do.

The helmet is a pretty self explanatory piece of armor. It was made of metal and covered soldiers' heads and faces. One wrong stab to the head would be certain death without a helmet.

helmet of salvation

Our minds control a lot. They control our actions. They control our confidence. They control our attitudes. Without the helmet of salvation, our minds are at risk of being infiltrated by the world and its lies. It is of utmost importance that we cover ourselves in reminders that Jesus died for us, that He loves us, that He is rooting for us, that He offers us grace and mercy and forgiveness no matter what.

This sword would have been a small, hand-held sword. It was one that soldiers would use in close quarters, not from a distance. Make no bones about it, though, it could still stab, wound, and kill.

The Sword of the Spirit is the Word of God. God's Word first and foremost "stabs" us. It is used to correct us and instruct us. However, God's Word is also an offensive tool for us to use in daily battle. When we memorize and read Scripture, the Holy Spirit brings its truths to our minds at the very moment we need them. His Word can certainly be used to make the enemy flee, but it is not so much meant to be a defensive tool against other believers.

sword of the spirit

So we've now covered 6 pieces of armor. But if you remember, we said that there were technically 7. Take a look at Ephesians 6:18 and record the first word here: _____.

Prayer. Oh yes! Friends, if we have on every piece of armor and totally neglect prayer, we are still in some serious trouble. Prayer helps us know when to fight and when to stand still. Prayer helps us to stay alert (vs. 18) so the enemy can't sneak in when we aren't watching. Prayer helps us to keep our focus others-ward as we pray for them to have the strength they need in their battles, too. Prayer helps us to know when to speak, how to speak, and what to speak just like Paul (vs. 20).

Grace Point

If you've watched <u>War Room</u>, you know the value of a quiet, prayer "closet." Find a quiet place to spend a few moments in prayer...even if that means moving from where you are right now.

Follow the ACTS prayer model to close out our time today:
<u>A</u>doration - Tell God what you love about Him
<u>C</u>onfession - Confess areas of sin to Him
<u>T</u>hanksgiving - Thank God for His blessings and Who He is
<u>S</u>upplication - Pray for the needs of others

DAY 4

We found Paul's final greeting to the Ephesians to be quite humorous. After 6 chapters of doctrine and theology and tough pills to swallow, he basically says he's going to send his friend to update the Ephesians on how he is doing and what he is doing.

We think you should read it. Hopefully, you'll find it as comical as we did. It just seems so anticlimactic.

Read Ephesians 6:21-24.

Did you feel like you were left hangin'? We sure did! Thankfully, this is not the only letter Paul wrote. We can glean more from him in his other letters: Romans, 1 & 2 Corinthians, Galatians, Philippians, Colossians, 1 & 2 Thessalonians, 1 & 2 Timothy, Titus, and Philemon. Go study those books to your heart's content. They're good!

For now, we'd like to leave you with our own Final Greetings.

Though I've walked with the Lord for many years now, grace has been something I've learned most recently. I'm a perfectionist with the best of them. I love a good checklist. Growing up, I basically saw quiet times as checklists. I gained much head knowledge from my times with Him, but in those times, my checklist mentality caused me to miss one of the greatest gifts He has given: grace. Maybe that is you, too.

Teacher friends, we have journeyed together for the past 7 weeks for one reason: to try to help you understand what Paul understood…that *Grace Changes Everything*. If it were not for grace, truly, where would I be? I'd be in the chains of legalism. I'd be bound to my "good" works. My chains would be made from my checklists that were never quite fulfilling for my heart and soul.

One of the hardest things in the world for me to do is receive gifts. Yep. You read that right. I'll give all day every day, but receiving is a different story. When the Lord began to strip away the legalistic chains, He showed me that I had to be ready and willing to receive a gift, His gift, grace. I don't receive it perfectly to this day. I often balk at my unworthiness. I often cringe at my lack of perfection. But God…but God looks at me through eyes of grace and love and forgiveness.

I don't know where the end of this study finds you, but I feel like at least one of you is like me. You beat yourself up for not being perfect. You tear yourself down with inner dialogue that would crush anyone if they could only hear the words you speak to yourself. You strive to check things off of a list because you believe that your worth is tied up in what you do, not in who you are. Sweet friend, those are chains. Paul has pleaded with you for 6 chapters to see that you are free - yes, free indeed.

As you go your way, would you be willing to use the key that is in your own hand - yep, you've had it the whole time! - to unlock the chains of the lies that have held you down? God is speaking grace over you. He loves you. He isn't condemning you. Romans 8:1 clearly tells us that "there is therefore now NO condemnation for those who are in Christ Jesus." Take a look at your feet. Are they bound, too? Do you feel stuck? It isn't your Father who has placed shackles on those feet of yours. He says in Romans 5:2 that we stand in GRACE. So…I wonder if, like me, you simply need to learn to receive gifts. His gifts. Rather than shying away from His gift, rather than leaving it unopened, open your hands and your heart to His grace.

I pray that God's abundant grace finds you right where you are today and that you feel the overflow of His love. I pray that you will receive what He made part of His inheritance for all of His children so long ago - grace. I pray that you will discover that grace truly changes everything…even for, no, especially for you.

Until next time,

Bethany

Over my desk hangs a Thomas Kinkade painting. No, not a real one. I wish. It is a canvas print of a lighthouse standing tall, shining its light onto a splashing ocean. When I was looking to purchase the Thomas KinKade print, I wanted to purchase one with a lighthouse. I ordered the print and waited weeks for its arrival. I had decided to give it as a gift to someone that I love dearly. As the gift was opened, I watched with awe as the gift's receiver sat and stared at each intricate detail in the painting. I was excited to give the gift, but the person to whom I had chosen to give the painting couldn't take his eyes off of each small minute detail. If you were to look at the picture, you might notice the crashing waves against the rocks on the sea's edge. You may notice the sunlight shining down on the red roofed cottage. A well-worn path is leading up to the small house. It makes you wonder who lives in such a place of beauty. There is a sail boat sailing in the distance. The sky has tints of pink, gold, and orange that shine through the gray, puffy clouds that billow up into the sky. Thomas Kinkade has a knack for painting details. His paintings are ones that you can sit and stare at for hours on end. There are new details that you can find each time you look at one of his paintings.

Growing up my mother always wanted me to share details of my day at school. I was an only child and plagued with the job of providing my dear mother with DETAILS. She wanted to know everything about my day and wanted me to start from the beginning and not leave out anything. To this day, I get phone calls from my mother, and I can hear her right now saying, "I want details! Start from the beginning, and don't leave anything out!"

I think Thomas Kinkade, my mother, and Paul had something in common. They loved details. Thomas Kinkade paints highly detailed pictures in which you can get lost. My mom wanted to know everything about my day. She knew that if she could hear all the details, she could take those moments to disciple my heart. Paul was very detailed in his writing to the Ephesians. Through his inspired words, he paints a beautiful picture of God's love, mercy, and grace. Paul was concerned with the details of the Ephesians' hearts just like God is concerned with the details of your heart.

I pray that this study has allowed you to open your heart and let God bring to light the details of sin that He has sufficiently covered with His GREAT GRACE. Grace changes the details of sin. Grace changes our hearts. *Grace Changes Everything.*

Grace and peace to you,

Bonnie Kathryn

Take a moment to sit and worship with our friend, Israel Houghton. Just sit and listen to him sing these truths over you..

GRACE IN THE CLASSROOM

Throughout this study, we have focused on God's grace. We would like to take a minute to provide you with some practical tips for displaying grace in your classroom whether you are in a public or private school.

1 **Take a moment to walk a mile in your students' shoes**. Imagine yourself spending a day in your classroom as the student. Think about the student with ADHD, autism, learning disabilities, behavioral struggles. What can you do as a teacher to help that student feel comfortable and blossom?

2 **Respond, do not react.** Oftentimes, we choose to react from emotion to certain situations. This causes outbursts of anger and hurtful words. When someone responds, she takes a moment to think about the most loving way to respond instead of having an immediate reaction. Practice the power of 10. Count to 10. Take 10 minutes. If the situation is HUGE, take 10 hours. Often, our responses will change if we take a moment to pray and think about how God would have us to respond.

3 **Go the extra mile.** Teachers often go the extra mile. It is just in our DNA. God made us that way. However, it is easy to withhold the EXTRAS from students who we feel don't deserve them. Grace means your class may be acting like a bunch of fools, yet you still choose to bring them brownies. This doesn't mean that you're supporting poor choices, but sometimes grace changes attitudes. It certainly changed our attitudes. We don't deserve the gift of salvation, "BUT GOD being rich in mercy because of the great love with which he loved us, even when we were dead in our trespasses made us alive together with Christ..."

4 **Always firmness, but with love.** Remember teacher number 3? She was the one who had high expectations that were clear for students. In elementary, this is the teacher whose class is on-task, meeting expectations without students having to ask a million questions. In high school, this is the classroom where students sit engaged and have appropriate dialogue with the teacher. Respect is evident. Grace is the balance between maintaining relationships and upholding procedures.

5 **Teaching to your students' needs.** With all the pressures of teaching, it is sometimes easier to teach the curriculum rather than students. Grace in the classroom is looking at each individual student and recognizing how they best learn and teaching them in a way that they will best understand. It means that you know that every child is not going to conform to one mode of teaching. Some need to move. Some need to talk. Some need to listen. Recognizing that each student is different, you find ways to engage and pique his or her interest.

Terms of Use

This item is for single classroom use only. Duplication for an entire school system or commercial purposes is strictly forbidden without written permission from the author. Copying any part of this product and placing it on the internet in any form (even a personal/classroom website) is strictly forbidden and is a violation of the Digital Millennium Copyright Act (DMCA).

Carter, J.W. *Redemption: Faith Without Compromise.* 2011. 18 4 2017. <http://www.biblicaltheology.com/eph/49_03_01.html>.

Henry, Matthew. *www.biblestudytools.com.* 1706. 30 April 2017. <http://www.biblestudytools.com/commentaries/matthew-henry-complete/>.

Shirer, Priscilla. *The Armor of God.* Nashville: LifeWay Press, 2015.

Unknown. *www.blb.org.* 2017. 30 April 2017. <https://www.blueletterbible.org>.

We would like to thank our pastors, J.D. Greear and Brett Marlowe, for their discipleship. We have gleaned much wisdom from their faithful study of God's Word and teaching.

Author Credits:
Bethany Fleming
Bonnie Hunter

Made in the USA
Coppell, TX
02 June 2020

26855324R00061